# I Say Nothing (3)

# I Say Nothing (3)

## My family and other puzzles

SANDY BALFOUR

**theguardian**

ATLANTIC BOOKS
LONDON

First published in Great Britain in 2006 by Atlantic Books
on behalf of Guardian Newspapers Ltd.

Atlantic Books is an imprint of Grove Atlantic Ltd.

1 2 3 4 5 6 7 8 9

A CIP catalogue record for this book is available from the British Library.

ISBN 10:  1 84354 517 9
ISBN 13:  978 1 84354 517 0


Printed in Great Britain

Atlantic Books
An imprint of Grove Atlantic Ltd
Ormond House
26–27 Boswell Street
London wc1n 3jz

# Contents

O TEMPORA, O MORES

# Anyone for Crosswords

Bill Clinton used to do crosswords. I wonder whether Tony Blair does? The idea has a quixotic appeal, a bit like the notion of President Bush, say, reading a novel. But I can't quite see it and Downing Street wouldn't say. Crosswords require patience and humour and a willingness to submit to the random and surreal orthography of the setter's mind. They do not, by and large, provide a home for control freaks. A crossword setter, Fawley once told me, is entering a game in which the point is to lose gracefully. By the same token the point for the solver is to win – appreciatively.

Like I say, Tony and Araucaria? I don't think so.

But if he did, he might feel that the *Guardian* setters were having a go at him. A couple of weeks back Paul was on the case with a very sarcastic 'What could be subtler during search for weapon! (7,4)'[i] It was a theme he started on some months ago. 'Say it aloud, sending ships to the Gulf was such a mistake – a build-up demanding contemplation (5,5),'[ii] for example.

It was no coincidence that this appeared in a puzzle in the *Guardian* on 15 February 2003, which alert readers will recall was the day news chiefs had been warned by the Pentagon to expect the second Gulf War to begin. In the same puzzle we found a number of other clues critical of Our Leader's enthusiasm for all things military.

Paul is not the only one. Three weeks ago Bunthorne weighed in with 'Spites Blix over possible arms sales, say? (7,7)'[iii] which could hardly be taken as a neutral comment on our ongoing imperial adventures. And last Saturday, Araucaria anticipated the government's discomfort over its statements on Iraq with his usual subtlety: 'Abjure blue berets? (5)'.[iv] Alistair Campbell must wish he could, literally and cryptically.

If things continue to slip in Iraq the Prime Minister would do well to heed Bunthorne's warning: 'Living with past record? Fail and "You will —!" (2,7)'.[v] I suspect that, despite the Iraqi failure to lose gracefully and the American inability to win appreciatively, the Prime Minister's place in history is secure.

But is it the one he wants?

18 AUGUST 2003

i CLUSTER BOMB; ii NAVEL FLUFF; iii VISIBLE EXPORTS; iv UNSET;
v BE HISTORY

## Tony Blair's Place in History

Following intelligence failures in Iraq, there has been much talk of 'blame' recently, which is what happens when real life intrudes on our carefully constructed semantic fantasies.

'Russian nouns decline,' I said before the storm broke last Wednesday.

'How many letters?' asked my girlfriend.

For some years she has been campaigning to get me to call out crossword clues properly. The 'proper' method is to say the number of letters first, then the clue, then any checked letters and then the number of letters again. It's a question of manners.

'It's not a clue,' I replied.

'What is it then?'

'Well, I don't know. I suppose you'd call it a "remark".'

'Oh.'

We were in bed at the time (sensitive readers may want to turn away at this point) and the sun was rising over London.

'What made you say that?'

I supposed I had said it because my Russian teacher had drummed it into us the previous evening. '*Today* we will *do* the *accusative*,' he said. He has a habit of stressing two or three words in every sentence, like a camp version of Graham Norton. 'The *accusative* is the *object* of the *sentence*. The *object* of the *exercise*, on the other *hand*, is that you will *learn* about *nouns*.'

The effect was to make me slightly seasick, bobbing about as I was on the choppy seas of his scansion. But you take my point. Never again in our house will a word be used as though it has only one meaning.

By breakfast therefore, storm clouds were gathering in the west.

'You don't understand how I feel,' said my girlfriend. I hesitate to say petulantly.

She wrested the newspaper from me and went to drink her coffee.

'You're imagining things,' I replied, not necessarily helpfully.

There was a silence, mostly in the accusative.

'I'm sure all I feel includes more than what I imagine,'[i] she said eventually.

But since she failed to call out the number of letters (which was 'four and four'), I had no way of knowing that this was not 'a remark', but a clue – taken from that morning's Cinephile puzzle in the *Financial Times*.

For which I blame her. Or him. Or anyone other than me.

25 JULY 2003

i REAL LIFE

---

# *The Hutton Inquiry*

There has been much made – in the *Guardian* particularly – of the different approaches taken by various media owners to the deliberations of Lord Hutton in the matter of the death of Dr Kelly. Commentators have suggested that some newspapers are motivated more by the political calculations of their proprietors than by any respect for what one might term 'the truth'.

Happily the crosswords setters (many of whom are, ah, promiscuous in their setting allegiance) have no truck with this sort of thing and it was possible to discern their maverick commentary on the Hutton inquiry in most of the papers. In the *FT* on Tuesday for example (atoning for a couple of repeated clues and solutions the previous day) Quark described 'How some went for attack lacking sense of proportion (4-3-3)'.[i]

But it was Rufus, normally the most amenable of setters, who seemed to be almost prescient on Monday. 'Something said about Anthony (6)'[ii] (or TB, as they seem to call him in the e-mails that fly around what the papers refer to as the 'upper echelons of Downing Street'), was clearly not something Alistair

Campbell was about to 'Let pass (6)',[iii] especially not given the 'Global degree of freedom (8)'[iv] enjoyed by the press and in particular by that 'Intriguing, if cruel, devil (7)',[v] the BBC.

Actually that last clue was from Wednesday's *Times*, a paper that has consistently supported the government (and anyone else) in its battles with the BBC. The setter, though, wanted to know whether there were 'Any left who'll get worried by inconspicuous observer? (3,2,3,4)'.[vi]

Not by the time they have finished with them. I have in my time been such an observer and know as well as any government apparatchik that it is not your presence that counts as much as what you say afterwards. Still, I did enjoy the extracts widely quoted. I wondered only that when Campbell described the government's evidence on 10 September as a 'detailed draft dossier', the papers forgot to mention that 'detailed' is an anagram of (amongst other things) 'dated lie'.

22 AUGUST 2003

i OVER-THE-TOP; ii REMARK;

iii PERMIT; iv LATITUDE; v LUCIFER;

vi FLY ON THE WALL

## *The Death of Stephen King?*

Is Stephen King OK? Has anyone heard? I only ask because Paul had a puzzle themed on the great man and his work on Tuesday and Paul's record in these matters is, ah, mixed. Screaming Lord Sutch, for example, passed away the moment Paul put him in a puzzle.

I feared the worst when I saw that this puzzle appeared the day after the National Book Club awarded King a lifetime achievement medal. The award is given to 'an American author who has enriched the literary landscape through a lifetime of service or body of work'. Previous recipients include Arthur Miller and Oprah Winfrey – and you may make of that what you will.

The difficulty – or the challenge – of a puzzle like this one is that one's ability to solve it depends in part on one's familiarity with the theme. I have not – as far as I know – read a Stephen King novel although I did once see the movie *Misery* on an aeroplane and so I found this one harder than usual. But not impossible. And in fact Stephen King was the last answer I filled in – and that was only because it fitted. It took a while longer (and some superior smiles from my girlfriend) before I worked out how you get his name from '"It" was one of his favourites, written up for a sort of party piece (7,4)'.

And that's the test. Good – which is to say fair – clueing should still allow the solver to get the answers, whether or not he knows the theme.

But back to Stephen King. There is something sinister about the phrase 'a lifetime of service'. It suggests that the life in question may be over … or almost over. And King is only fifty-six years old. He is reported to have said that he will donate the $10,000 that comes with the medal to the National Book Foundation. But the medal, he said, 'I will keep and treasure for the rest of my life.'

Which will be long and happy, I trust.

19 SEPTEMBER 2003

# Duffers

You see them hanging around the centres of our cities on a Saturday night: shifty-looking young men with the word 'duffer' emblazoned across their chests. I had hitherto thought this to be a surprisingly honest admission on the part of the wearers, rather than a fashion statement. I was raised, you see, with Arthur Ransome's maxim ringing in my ears: 'Better drowned than duffers. If not duffers won't drown,' was Commander Walker's encouraging response to the suggestion that his children should go sailing on their own in *Swallows and Amazons*. But – having solved last week's prize puzzle by Taupi – I now realize that these hooded youths are part of a crack unit of crossword setters, specializing in anagrams.

'Sailor's shanty: "MacDuff" (9)'[i] was the clue. My son was, at the time, prancing about the living room with a plastic sword telling his sisters to 'Lay on, MacDuff,' and it took me a while to get past Macbeth and realise that what we were dealing with was an anagram. But was it legitimate? There is occasional debate in crossword circles as to whether clues like 'Ancient Hindu in a jiffy (4)'[ii] in which the indicator – 'iffy' – is part of another word, can be allowed. I'm in favour, but find it harder to answer the question of, 'How much movement/change must the word suggest to be a legitimate anagram indicator?' In this case, I suppose 'pudding' would be acceptable, especially as 'duff' in this sense was a term commonly used by seamen, which gave the clue a nice symmetry.

But 'duff', I discover, has much more to offer than that, both as a noun and a verb. A duffer may duff his duff while sitting on duff covered in duff, which is to say a 'worthless fool' may 'alter the appearance of' his 'buttocks' while sitting on 'a bed of decaying leaves' covered in 'fine coal dust'. What a word! Best of all, in Australia it can mean to alter the branding on stolen cattle.

Perhaps those young men are not crossword fanatics after all.

17 OCTOBER 2003

i YACHTSMAN; ii JAIN

## *England Wins the Rugby World Cup*

You know winter is here when cricket clues seem to be fewer and further between and in their stead our National Winter Sport rears its ugly head.

My friend Andy is not a crossword person, but he does take a passing interest in my world in much the same way as I tease him each time Tottenham Hotspur lose. I was pleased therefore to be able to show him Paul's puzzle last Friday in which we found 'At Portsmouth, then another team (9,7)'.[i] Even then he didn't get it. Spurs' run of form has been so bad of late that he couldn't believe anyone would put them in a puzzle. On the same day (perhaps by coincidence) Dac in the *Independent* put out a rival clue in the form of 'Football team seen half-heartedly taking dip in sea (7)'.[ii] And even the *Financial Times*, a newspaper whose sports coverage is not famously lavish, was at it. Neo's clue did at least reveal a certain distaste for football, or for the current version of it where only three teams have a chance at the title: 'City game unfinished in cheerless season (10)'.[iii]

Of course, now that England's National Winter Sport is in danger of being booed off, stage left, by the New Official Home Counties (and Newcastle) Winter Sport, we may soon witness a rash of rugby-related clues. The sport is not, I think, as linguistically fertile as cricket, but there is no doubt that words like 'ruck', 'maul' and 'conversion' will crop up regularly as anagram indicators and various players will get to see their names in print. Whether Neil Back can, like Pele, become a regular feature of puzzles remains to be seen. But for the assistance of those not familiar with the England rugby team's goal-scoring tactics, I offer the following advice.* In any clue containing one or more of these words: 'razor', 'close shave', 'sword' or 'Messiah', the answer is 'Wilkinson'.

This holds true until, oh, 2007, at which point things may or may not be different.

* Offer valid only in England.

5 DECEMBER 2003

i TOTTENHAM HOTSPUR; ii ARSENAL; iii WINCHESTER

---

## *Iraqi 'Freedom'*

The late Hunter S. Thompson is reported to have said of television that it is 'a cruel and shallow money trench, a long plastic hallway where thieves and pimps run free, and good men die like dogs.' According to an article in *Newsweek* at the weekend, the same could be said of the new Iraq in which drugs, prostitution and pornography are rife. According to Iraqis quoted in the article, these new features of everyday life in Baghdad represent 'the bad side of freedom'. I have spent much of the past year in the United States where other unhappy sides – or side effects – of freedom were all too obvious, particularly the number of people damaged by guns and the numbers of people suffering from obesity.

In the media white noise following the arrest of Saddam Hussein 'at 8.30 p.m. local' it was possible within the reporting of the event to discern a number of undercurrents around which a consensus had clearly not yet been reached. Most obviously the question of where Saddam should face trial which, depending who was talking at the time, may or may not have been the same question as whether or not he should face the death penalty.

As always I found much to interest me in the details. The reported presence of Mars Bar wrappers, for example, was eerily reminiscent of those accounts of Adolf Hitler in the bunker in April 1945, by which time he is now known to have subsisted almost exclusively on a bottomless diet of chocolate cake.

But I also caught a remark at the weekend on one of the news channels. It was said off camera and indeed I could not see the speaker, whom I took to be an American soldier talking to an Iraqi reporter. The soldier was trying to be helpful.

'Well, just ask,'[i] he was heard to say, and it was only when I did Paul's puzzle on Tuesday that I wondered for how many Iraqi women the answer to this clue to a seven letter word will now be the career path of freedom.

19 DECEMBER 2003

i SOLICIT

# Beckham (1)

To Turin this week, where I am engaged in the process that is a tragedy to those who feel, and a comedy to those who think – otherwise known as television production. It was, I decided on the flight over here, time for me to grow up – at least in crossword terms. With some trepidation therefore, I folded back the page at what has previously proved to be my crosswording limit: the Azed puzzle in the *Observer*. It was one of his 'plain' ones, which is to say that I had a passing chance of solving at least two clues, and I set to it with a will.

Well, I say 'with a will'. Twenty minutes and one solution later I found my eyes straying to the *Mail on Sunday*, which one of the stars of our new show was reading beside me. I have only the most passing acquaintance with this newspaper, but I was intrigued to read its page-three story ('Nice Tackle David') in which, after an evening at the 'exclusive Nobu restaurant' (whom or what does it exclude?), Victoria Beckham was photographed with her hand on her husband's crotch.

Well, I ask you! How can crosswords possibly compete with such diversions? The article helpfully (for those of us who didn't get the point) told us that Mrs Beckham calls him 'Goldenballs' and that the couple live in a £3 million home 'dubbed Beckingham Palace'. There was some speculation too as to whether or not she was checking to see if he was wearing one of her thongs, another thing he 'famously' did. Or does. Who knows? Who cares?

Thinking, in that sense, that I had learned nothing from this, ah, interlude, I returned to the more sedate waters of the Azed puzzle... only to find that suddenly it started to make sense.

There is a prize for solving it, and so I can't give the answer, but in the world of the *Mail on Sunday*, 34 across goes without saying: 'Fashion in sport isn't silly for today's artistic reactionary (13)'.[i]

16 JANUARY 2004

i POSTMODERNIST

---

## One Word, Trois Mots

A few years ago at the United Nations in New York there was a conference of sorts that began the successful political process which has brought a degree of stability and – who knows? – even peace to the (as yet anything but) Democratic Republic of Congo. The event was chaired by a very senior French diplomat who gave me a moment of amusement with the slight miscount in his final injunction to the delegates. 'As you return to your countries,' he said in French, 'remember these three words, "La paix, la paix, la paix".'

But the delegates went forth, and now the DRC has a government consisting of most of the previously warring parties and the real prospect of elections at some not too distant point. In the meantime the UN forces, called MONUC, act as nursemaid to the peace.

The surface reading for 9 across by Aelred in the *Independent* last Tuesday therefore seemed a little harsh, although the clue itself was pleasingly coherent: 'Peacekeepers under canvas charge friendly power without meaning to (15)'.[i]

On the same day Paul managed to put a little more edge into another clue using the United Nations. Tuesday was, of course, a different era, back when it seemed possible that Tony Blair would be deposed by the twin threats of a backbench revolt and the findings of the Hutton inquiry. 'Entry into Baghdad wasn't about overthrowing of government, so has come apart (9)'.[ii]

Well, perhaps. Clues like this can drive the unwary solver (myself included) to distraction. It looked and felt too much like an anagram and I confess that I spent a moment longer than I would have liked trying to make something of 'so has come'. After all, the letter count was right, and 'apart' was perfectly serviceable as an anagram indicator.

But, as I say, that was a different era. In the new age of Blair, Paul's cry of frustration in 9 down seemed more likely to reflect the current mood of the nation: 'What do you want from us, Tony Blair? Give over! (13)'.[iii]

30 JANUARY 2004

i UNINTENTIONALLY; ii UNCOUPLED;

iii GOVERNABILITY

## *Miracle Transformations*

Some years ago, still relatively new to this country, I found myself at a dinner party at which the name of Bamber Gascoigne came up. 'Bamber who?' I asked. Despite the early success of *University Challenge*, he was not someone whose fame had extended to the warmer climes from which I hail. I was duly put in the picture (as well as my place) by my friends, and the next day a gift-wrapped edition of Bamber Gascoigne's *Encyclopaedia of Britain* arrived at my door. For more than a decade now this book has had pride of place in our loo, and it sometimes seems to me that the extent to which I am successfully 'integrated' (© D. Blunkett, 2004) is because I spend five minutes a day immersed in Gascoigne's book.

Gascoigne has, of course, been replaced by Jeremy Paxman and last Saturday I took my daughter to a recording of *University Challenge* in Manchester, in which the wise heads of the British Library were pitted against four crossword compilers, including the *Guardian*'s Bunthorne, Paul and Araucaria. The episode will not be shown until April and I shall not reveal who won.\* Seeing Paxman in action, however, did remind me of his award-winning interview – can it really be seven years ago? – with the Right Honourable Michael Howard MP.

Which brings me to the issue of the day: I have good news for the Conservative Party. No doubt they have their own pollsters giving them the numbers, but I would suggest that a far more reliable indication that replacing Iain Duncan Smith with Michael Howard has been a success is the fact that the great man has appeared not once but twice in the *Guardian* crossword in recent weeks. So much of modern politics is about name recognition. But there is a sting in the tale (*sic*): both Araucaria on Wednesday ('One, who had miracle to work – not all day, it was said (7,6)'[i]) and Paul three weeks ago ('Right man who had miracle transformation? (7,6)'[i]) recognised that the anagram of the Conservative leader's name is also a description of the magnitude of his transformation – and his task.

* The British Library by a considerable margin!

12 MARCH 2004

i MICHAEL HOWARD

## *The Road to Hell*

The idea of a politician carrying the can has a kind of visceral appeal, so much so that we often don't mind how it happens. But it seems to me that of all the prominent men and women of the past few years, with the possible exceptions of Mandela and Aung San Suu Kyi, one more exempt than most from such scrutiny is Vaclav Havel, former President of the Czech Republic. I have been unable to find any reference to him being someone who does crosswords, but I was browsing in one of his books – *Disturbing the Peace* – at the weekend, and it seemed to me he just might.

'Hope is definitely not the same thing as optimism,' he said in 1986. 'It is not the conviction that something will turn out well, but the conviction that something makes sense, regardless of how it turns out.'

Well! A solver's charter if ever I read one, and the sort of thing one needs to bear very much in mind when settling down to a puzzle by, say, Enigmatist. Actually, I tried the Enigmatist puzzle last Saturday with a conspicuous lack of success, but I retain my conviction that it will – when the solution is published

– all make sense. Bunthorne on Tuesday was better – which is to say I could do most of it: 'Politician and dramatist have left following holiday, carrying the can (6,5)'.[i]

It is now more than a year [February 2003] since Havel exited, stage left, from the frontline of Czech politics. At home – as is so often the case – his reputation is more mixed than it is abroad. The Czech right, for example, despise him for 'losing' Slovakia and others condemned him for his fondness for holding meetings in pubs. The drink never got him, but cancer nearly did, for he was many things, but never a puritan. And even if he doesn't do crosswords, I am sure that he would understand what Araucaria meant on Wednesday: 'Devoted to health, no? Word is, antiphlogistine will be needed (3,4,2,4,2,5,4,4,10)'.[ii]

Do not lose hope. It all makes sense…

2 APRIL 2004

i VACLAV HAVEL; ii THE ROAD TO HELL IS
PAVED WITH GOOD INTENTIONS

## *Self Portraits*

The democratic impulse takes many forms. Earlier this week I was in the National Portrait Gallery admiring the extraordinary exhibition of postcards collected over the years by Tom Phillips. Whimsically catalogued by subject matter – 'Two men', 'Aspidistra' and 'Charabancs', for example – the exhibition is entitled 'We are the People' and shows, as one visitor wrote in the messages book provided by the gallery, all 'the sad, slow music of humanity'. And so we saw shopkeepers and dancers, false seasides and real factories, families posed and relaxed, with babies awake or asleep. There were dancers, patriarchs and athletes, and in one particularly charming set there were hairdos to die for – and some to die from.

And yet it was not the pictures that held my attention, but the book of comments. Here visitors from across the country – and the world – had written their response to the exhibition. A surprising number had been moved to doodle or even elaborately sketch their own likenesses. Many commented on the sense of impending recognition, the expectation that they would at any moment walk around the corner and see themselves or their parents. We each scanned the faces and the backgrounds looking for something or someone that we might recognise as our own. Indeed one visitor had. 'My father recognised his father in the mill,' he wrote and went on to draw a diagram of where in the exhibition we might find the postcard of the mill with its workers, and where we too might see his father's father and think of him, perhaps, as our own.

Others had simpler questions to pose. 'Why no cats?' illustrates neatly the quixotic unpredictability of each response. Well, why not? I, of course, saw the parallel with crosswords, where each clue, each witticism, each word elicits from the solver an intensely personal and yet universal response.

On Wednesday Taupi came up with a beautifully constructed clue: 'Quandary of less civilized people in a flutter (12)'.[i] Or as someone wrote in the comments book on 4 March: 'I don't know what aspidistra or charabanc is. Please explain.'

7 MAY 2004

i BEWILDERMENT

# Spooks

Souers, Vandenberg, Hillenkoetter, Smith, Dulles, McCone, Raborn, Helms, Schlesinger, Colby, Bush, Turner, Casey, Webster, Gates, Woolsey, Deutch, Tenet*... Can you spot the connection? All famous men in their own field, but as a group they would not normally be of interest to crossword setters or solvers. To achieve that distinction you must have something a little more.

Christine Keeler, for example, made it into the most recent Brummie in the form of this clue: 'One about to be dubbed Christine "Cuddles" Knight (7)',[i] and only yesterday Gordius thought it not unreasonable that we should equate 'Harris' with 'Rolf'. In the same clue he used the much older crossword convention of having 'Lawrence' to indicate 'TE'. And everyone now knows that Britney Spears is an anagram of 'Presbyterians'. Perhaps it is wrong to say that you must have 'a little more'. President Bush, after all, is a reasonably frequent visitor to the *Guardian* and other crosswords. Tim Moorey, setting in the *Week*, has now published two very funny puzzles themed on 'Bushisms'. The president offers setters other opportunities. 'Lurking, one man rising against the President (2,6)'[ii] Gordius said yesterday.

Back to the list. These are the former and current directors of the Central Intelligence Agency since it was signed into existence in 1947 by President Truman. They are men who by and large do not choose to be in the public eye, although they might play up the post once they have left, particularly if, say, they are running for election. Even the present incumbent, who is one of the few – perhaps the only – senior officials from the Clinton era to prosper in the new dispensation, is not that well known. Perhaps 'prosper' is not the right word; 'survive' might be closer to the mark. Recent years have not been the CIA's finest hour. And he makes it into puzzles because his name is a palindrome. Rufus spotted this on Monday: 'Principle of having it both ways (5)',[iii] but it was Araucaria the previous week who gave the name that little extra gloss: 'Belief in the CIA is reversible (5)'.[iii]

* Tenet announced his resignation two weeks after this article appeared. He was held by many to be responsible for 'intelligence failures' in Iraq.

21 MAY 2004

i KNEELER; ii IN AMBUSH; iii TENET

---

# *Marco Polo*

'Ye Emperors, Kings, Dukes, Marquises, Earls, and Knights, and all other people desirous of knowing the diversities of the races of mankind, as well as the diversities of kingdoms, provinces, and regions of all parts of the East, read through this book and ye will find in it the most marvellous characteristics of the people especially of Armenia, Persia, India and Tartary...'

It sounds like the introduction to a book of crosswords, but actually it is the prologue to the *Travels of Marco Polo*, recently reissued by Liveright, which I have been reading this week. Perhaps it is only that he dictated the work while in prison following the defeat of the Venetian fleet, but Polo appears to have been a somewhat dour and humourless young man, primarily concerned with making money. And yet, almost despite himself, he managed to write one of the most gripping travel books of all time.

Which brings me to crosswords. It has never been entirely clear to me why the Azed puzzle in the *Observer* is hidden away in the travel – sorry 'Escape' – section of the newspaper. Perhaps it is just that you need to go on a very long journey to have a hope in Hades of completing one. Or perhaps – a more charitable view – it is that each puzzle itself represents a form of long-distance mental travel.

For Polo, of course, making money was inextricably tied up with keeping on the right side of Kublai Khan, about whom he waxes lyrical but who was anything but the 'fine upstanding Emperor that Marco Polo would have us believe'. This comes from the introduction to the new edition, written by Manuel Komroff, who goes on to describe Khan as a 'crafty schemer', 'hated by many of his subjects' who only 'held the throne by sheer force'.

Well, you wouldn't necessarily guess that from what Polo has to say. But then he was engaged in the business (I use the word advisedly) of so many travel writers which, as Azed put it, is to 'Forge complex myths about the ego (6)'.[i]

9 JULY 2004

i SMITHY

# How to Catch a Bear

In preparation for a trip to the far eastern edge of Siberia later this summer I have been reading Stepan Krasheninnikov's classic work of scientific discovery, *Explorations of Kamchatka 1735–1741*. Krasheninnikov was assigned to work as a botanist on Vitus Bering's second Kamchatka expedition in the 1730s, but he soon showed such aptitude for all manner of sciences that he was permitted to follow his own interests. After Bering (he of the Straits) died, Krasheninnikov spent nearly three years travelling Kamchatka on his own. It took ten years to record his findings and the work was published in 1755. It remains a model of scholarly precision and ambition.

One paragraph remains with me. Describing various ways in which native Kamchadals hunted bears, Krasheninnikov writes 'They attach a large block of wood to a rope with a running knot at the end. They place the block on the bear's trail. The bear feels the rope tighten, and he moves forward a little and realizes that the wood is hindering him. The bear becomes furious, pulls the massive piece behind, and drags it up to some high spot, where he takes the wood into his paws and throws it as hard as he can. The weight of the wood topples the bear. He falls headfirst and kills himself.'

Except sometimes he doesn't. Writing in the *Independent on Sunday* last week, Andrew Rawnsley helpfully listed the many large blocks of wood that the Prime Minister's enemies, (and friends, if you include Peter Mandelson) have attached to his legs since he came to power. Often we have seen him climb the nearest cliff, usually in the form of an inquiry, seemingly with every intention of throwing the log and therefore himself on to the rocks below. And yet he lives.

Much has been written on how he manages it. I would comment only that he must eventually fall victim to the phenomenon described by Gordius as 'What lies between government and electorate (11,3)'.[i]

For, as Krasheninnikov concludes, 'If the bear does not die the first time, he repeats this activity until he is dead.'*

* At the time this books went to press, the bear was alive and (possibly) well.

23 JULY 2004

# The Loveliest Girl in the Lake District

Tom Lehrer introduces his tribute to Alma Mahler-Werfel by describing her obituary as the 'juiciest, spiciest, raciest' it has ever been his pleasure to read. Here was a woman who had bedded most of the leading creative men of her time, amongst whom there were three 'whom she went so far as to marry'. Her story, according to Lehrer, was the stuff of which ballads should be made and, as was his way, he had composed a modest example.

I mention this only because two weeks ago Audreus gave us the most gloriously convoluted clue it has ever been my pleasure to see. I repeat it here for the record only; solvers will recognise it immediately and non-solvers will raise their eyebrow in the manner of one saying, 'See, I told you these puzzles were ridiculous.'

Take a deep breath: 'In which the disappearance of a non-celebrity leads to the poet's transmogrification (3,5,7 and few could 4,4,4,6,2,2 but 3 is 2,3,5 and, oh, the 10 to 10)'.[i]

'Come again?' said my girlfriend, lapsing into the South African idiom I thought she had lost, but to which we both resort in moments of stress.

I came again, so to speak, to no avail. But the best approach to these sorts of clues is to get as many checked letters as possible. Soon we had sufficient letters to get the pattern for the first three words.

Wordsworth's 'Lucy' poems have stirred much critical debate over the years, but what is not in question is their power to move the reader. Lucy may well have been 'A Maid whom there were none to praise/ And very few to love,' but her memory lingers on in our poetry and the puzzles of our newspapers and that seems to me a more fitting claim to fame than that of the loveliest girl in Vienna.

10 SEPTEMBER 2004

i The solution comes from this stanza: 'SHE LIVED UNKNOWN, and few could KNOW/WHEN LUCY CEASED TO BE;/ But SHE is IN HER GRAVE, and oh/ The DIFFERENCE to me!' Except that for 'me' read 'WORDSWORTH'

## Beckham (2)

The dubious claims on our attention this week of young Master Beckham have not as yet troubled the crossword setters of the

*Guardian.* As a breed (in my experience) they tend to be above the sort of celebrity shenanigans in which he indulges and, indeed, to have their eyes fixed on horizons more distant than the events of the moment. But, from time to time, puzzles of topical interest appear.

Of course it is easier if the topicality can be seen coming from a great distance. Readers will recall Pasquale's puzzle of two weeks ago in which he paid tribute to the late Graham Greene on the 100th anniversary of the author's birth. And a few weeks before that Araucaria drew our attention to the forthcoming season of the Kent Opera, now in the third year of its resurrection. From time to time, however, setters can do more than that. John Perkin, the former crossword editor of the *Guardian*, took great delight in telling me how, at the time of South Africa's first proper elections in 1994, he had to 'hold the back page' when Araucaria at the last moment had the idea of doing a puzzle in tribute to the leaders of the country's struggle for national liberation.

Different papers do it differently. *The Times* does not approve, for instance, of using the names of living persons in its puzzles and it is true that there have been times when there was an uncomfortable proximity between the name of a famous person appearing in a puzzle and the death of the person named. It happened in 1999 when Paul set a puzzle themed on party leaders and included this clue: 'Tories crush GLC; damn cheeky of party leader (9,4,5)'[i]... and in his tribute to Graham Greene, Pasquale managed to fit in another great thinker of our age: 'Philosopher completed article about sin (7)'.[ii]

I do not know the policy of the *Independent* in these matters, but I know which famous person came immediately to mind when I saw this clue by Columba on Tuesday: 'Tactless idiot going after credit (5)'.[iii]

15 OCTOBER 2004

i SCREAMING LORD SUTCH; ii DERRIDA; iii CRASS

---

# Gambling for Beginners

I know it is unfashionable to quote Polonius, but I'm going to do it anyway. This comes from the Virgilius puzzle – a setter I have not previously met – in last Monday's *Independent*: 'Deliberately took some of Polonius' advice? (5)'.[i]

But first: I well recall a warm night last January when my brother and I wandered through the parking lot of the Suncoast Casino in Durban, South Africa. We were nearing the end of a long day researching the city's dark underbelly for a novel for which I have as yet to type the first word... The flophouses of the Point Road, the biker bars of the Bluff, the all-night traders selling anything and anyone beneath the canopy of the motorway, and the desolate corners of the docks where, far from the lights of the Yacht Club or the Container Terminals, winos grunted amidst rust and broken glass...

By comparison, of course, the casino was meant to represent all that is bright and hopeful, with its pastel colours and 'welcome' signs. Ten years ago the new South Africa went through the debates on gambling that this government has only now initiated. There, as everywhere, the neon lights beckoned, and casinos were built. That night my brother and I paused in the parking lot to do a count of the children abandoned to sleep (except not all were sleeping, merely crying) in the parked cars while their parents gambled away their futures. One child would have been too many and there was more than one.

We were accosted by a gambler seeking funds. No, we would not give him any, so he renegotiated. Perhaps we could lend him R500? He would pay us back in an hour. With interest. He was onto a winner, or would be soon. He was sure of it.

Of course we took Polonius' advice, but I remember leaving that dismal, deathly place with the conviction that those who argue in favour of casinos have either never been to one, or are succumbing to a set of interests other than the public one.

29 OCTOBER 2004

i LENTO

## *Our Four-Legged Friends*

Earlier this week I sat in my favourite position beneath the Tumulus on Hampstead Heath and watched the orange dawn spread its wings across London. I don't do this as often as I used to. Wisdom or sloth or the prospect (however remote) of a nice cup of tea militate against it.

But on Tuesday I rose early and headed for the hills. It's a wonderful time of day, one's only company the crows and rabbits, and a couple of men who sleep rough near the south meadow. I'm on nodding terms with one, but tend to avoid the other. We haven't been close since he nicked my newspaper – with a half-completed Taupi, what's more – to make himself a bed.

Groping through my pockets I found a clue from last week's *Sydney Morning Herald*. A reader in New Zealand (this crossword world gets smaller and smaller!) sent it to me because it contained an extended anagram, which was, he said, one of the best he had ever seen. 'Me, cats or dogs and so on with rightful human risk? I warn otherwise (2,6,3,4,6,3,6,2,4,9)'.[i]

Without any checked letters it was hard to know where to begin. In any case my attention was held by an early morning fox as it stole across the path. Perhaps thirty metres from me it froze. So did I, although it was not me that held the fox's attention, but something rustling in the grass. For several minutes I sat and watched as the hunter and the hunted crouched in fear and expectation. But the mouse must have reached its burrow, for the fox turned back its ears, looked disdainfully at me and moved on.

I couldn't do the clue in the end. I had to ask for the solution – but at least I can say that what was true for the setting was true for the solving.

16 MARCH 2005

i NO ANIMAL WAS HURT DURING THE MAKING OF THIS CROSSWORD

## *Your Majesty (sort of)*

Our friend arrives like a thoroughbred horse by way of Schiphol out of Curaçao. The tags on his bags say things like 'Kampala' and 'San Juan'. His brow is furrowed. His handshake is clammy and he has the distant and hunted look of a man engaged in Very Important Business for some government or other. In his jetlag and fatigue he doesn't say much; like the message in a bottle, he has been afloat on the seas too long to be easily opened up.

But my girlfriend is good at this sort of thing. She embraces him warmly and puts the kettle on. She asks after his family (they're well) and wonders whether he regrets letting his son have his ears pierced (he had no choice). She hopes the school thing is working out (it is), and shares a memory or two about common friends.

She wonders what brings him here.

At which he gives an involuntary start. His hand strays towards his Blackberry. 'I just need to check something,' he says and he starts scrolling through e-mails and flight schedules. He's making travel plans. He asks about trains to Windsor. He moans about the unfortunate business of the Pope's funeral. He wonders, perhaps, could he stay another night?

And suddenly I realise what's bothering him. Like so many people inconvenienced by the week's events, including Prince Charles and his bride, he's having to reschedule. By way of consolation I offer him last week's *Private Eye* which contained the most scurrilous, rude and thoroughly delightful puzzle it has ever been my pleasure to solve. One small sample from the slew of unmitigated smut: 'Camilla at present is second-rate shag – time to get an honour? (5-2-2)'.[i]

She is today, but she won't be tomorrow, whether or not my friend is there.

08 April 2005

i BRIDE-TO-BE

# An Election Looms

My son is much taken with the idea that it is possible in the election next week to give Tony Blair and his government a bloody nose. Bloody noses are a regular (though not frequent) feature of life in the playgrounds of north London and the idea that it is both legitimate and highly desirable to thump Tony Blair (if only metaphorically) appeals to him.

He likes it even more that he understands the reason. In his world 'He lied to me', is more than sufficient cause for the inadvertent bump that sends the liar tumbling to the ground where he will not only get a bloody nose but quite possibly a scraped knee as well.

But he wonders if it is enough? Bloody noses soon dry up. A few dabs with a tissue, a couple of splashes of water, a pat on the back and the bleeder is soon restored to their former position within the group.

I say this only because I know that as the nation's premier political pundit it is my solemn duty (on this historic occasion) to tell you how to vote. For this purpose I have decided that it is probably in everyone's interest if I eschew the usual broadsheet technique of reasoned argument and thoughtful political analysis and opt instead to model this column on the leader columns of the tabloids.

Which is harder than it looks, but here goes.

The current lot are a bunch of mendacious cowards! The Tories are rubbish! The Liberal who? The X-Philes says (or is it 'say'?) why not vote for a 'New Party? (5)'.[i]

Do it early, though only once.

29 APRIL 2005

i GREEN by Araucaria.

## *How the Ashes Weren't Won*

It is (though probably only briefly) a tough time to be Australian.* And so at the cricket club for which I play there has been much rejoicing at events at the Rose Bowl on Monday and in Taunton on Wednesday.

But it is tinged with the recognition that we have all been there. Last Sunday was a case in point. We were due a win and our tactics were simple: win the toss, elect to bat, make a bunch of runs in our forty overs and then scuttle the opponents out with 100 or so runs to spare. It worked for our opponents the week before – and for England on Monday – so why not for us?

Well, because it didn't. Eleven balls later we had five runs on the board and four batsmen back in the pavilion. And four of our five runs were wides. It was carnage.

At this point our skipper joined me at the crease. He is a cultured man and does the crossword from time to time. What was required, he said, was a 'Length of time in the middle (10)'.[i] But his first ball struck him on the pads. Now the trouble with LBW decisions at this level of cricket is that the batting side supplies the umpires. So when the appeal goes up, you have to decide whether or not to give your teammate out. Obviously the answer is 'no' – but sometimes umpires say 'yes'.

Make that five back in the pavilion.

It's the sort of mistake anyone can make. The ball is straight, it hits the pads and before you think what you're doing, you've given the skipper out and are left wondering whether this will be your 'Last appearance in a home game (5)'.[ii]

\* In the triangular one-day tournament Australia were beaten first by Bangladesh and then England.

17 JUNE 2005

i CENTIMETRE by Rufus; ii OMEGA by Quantum.

# A Chocolate Diversion

When I consider how my life is spent, my thoughts turn inevitably to chocolate. You'll be pleased to know that when they gather for their deliberations in Gleneagles, the leaders of our free (though not necessarily fair) world will find a bar of Divine chocolate on their pillows at night. It is all part of the hospitality provided by Her Majesty's Government. I wonder if they will like it. I wonder if they will read the label?

Because if they did, of course, they might be led to ponder on where the money goes. If your bar of chocolate in the super-market costs £1, the first seventeen pence (more or less) go to HM Customs and Excise in the form of VAT. Of the remaining eighty-three pence, perhaps twenty-five pence goes to the supermarket. Roughly twenty pence is non-cocoa ingredients, eight pence is manufacturing, packaging and transport costs. Another twenty-five pence belongs to the company that owns the brand and markets the chocolate. By my calculation that leaves only five pence to pay for the cocoa.

You have to eat a lot of chocolate to make Africans rich on that. And in the process several European industries (and the government) will get considerably richer. If our aim is to enrich the lives of Africans through trade (and I hope it is) , it would be better if, say, we all bought chocolate in which the brand – and the twenty-five pence profit margin that goes with it – is owned by African cocoa growers. This was certainly my thinking when I helped establish Divine chocolate and it remains an idea to which I am 'Fully committed, like ships engaged in free trade? (2,5,6)'.[i]

Well, perhaps not *quite* like them!

1 JULY 2005

i NO HOLDS BARRED by Rover.

# Ol' Man River

The floods caused by Hurricane Katrina reminded me that I once spent a few weeks in New Orleans making a film about the power of the Mississippi and the likelihood that the city would one day no longer be – what was the word? – feasible. At that time the perceived threat was from the north rather than the south, and the expectation was that the city, rather than being flooded, would be left dry as the Mississippi took a shorter and steeper route to the sea. The river changes direction every 10,000 years or so. The next major shift is due around about now. Experts suggest that the likely breaking point is at Old River, a few miles upstream from Baton Rouge. It is here that the river threatens to turn right and pour itself into the Atchafalaya Basin. If that happens, New Orleans will no longer have the river on which it depends, and under whose threat it lives.

Old River is a little further upriver than Angola, the home of the Louisiana State Penitentiary and 5,000 inmates, roughly half of whom are there 'for life'. Like New Orleans, Angola is surrounded on three sides by the Mississippi and protected by an inherently unstable system of levees.

One morning soon after dawn we took a helicopter ride up the river from Baton Rouge with a view to filming before the light got too hard and brittle. But at Angola the pilot came on the intercom to beg our patience. 'There's just something I gotta do,' he said. I watched the altimeter as we rose above the prison and then, with a sudden lurch, began to drop rapidly towards the central courtyard. I could see guards reaching for their firearms, when the pilot suddenly pulled the helicopter up and we peeled away towards the river.

'Just saying hello,' he said. 'My brother's in there for killing a guy.'

Yesterday there were television pictures of prisoners stuck by the floodwaters against the roofs of their holding pens, a reminder that in times of disaster it is all too easy to forget, 'Those who've gone off with life-changing rabble (3,4,3,4)'.[i]

2 SEPTEMBER 2005

i THE RANK AND FILE

# Hedging and Hogging

For reasons that escape me I have been rereading Isaiah Berlin's essay, 'The Hedgehog and the Fox' in which he discusses 'Tolstoy's view of History'. It beats Sudoku, you understand.

Berlin's essay gets its name from a fragment of the Greek poet Archilocus which says, 'The fox knows many things, but the hedgehog knows one big thing'. As Berlin points out, this is open to many interpretations. It may just be that 'the fox, for all his cunning' is defeated by the hedgehog's one defence. But Berlin thinks there is more to it, even that the words 'can be made to yield a sense in which they mark one of the deepest differences which divide writers and thinkers and, it may be, human beings.'

And what is this difference? On one side there are those who 'relate everything to a single vision' in terms of which they 'understand, think and feel.' On the other side are those who 'pursue many ends, often unrelated and even contradictory... their thought is scattered or diffused, moving on many levels, seizing upon the essence of a vast array of experiences and objects for what they are in themselves.' And doing so without trying to fit them into some 'at times fanatical, unitary inner vision.'

Dante belonged to the first group and Shakespeare to the second. But which was Tolstoy? And which applies best to those who set crosswords – and to those who solve them?

I have neither the space nor the erudition to offer a sensible answer to this question, but I suspect that – as Berlin said of

Tolstoy – we are by nature mostly foxes, although we hide it well. For we all too easily find comfort in being hedgehogs. In these troubled times we are to seek shelter in a 'fanatical, unitary inner vision' of the sort articulated by our Prime Minister. But really our strength – and I think now of the city I call home – lies in our ability simultaneously to 'pursue many ends, unrelated and even contradictory.' Fractured, diverse, chaotic and splendid, like a good crossword clue.

5 AUGUST 2005

# THE ITALIAN FOR LOVE

## Take Five

I am in Turin where my fellow producer and I swap stories and wait for things to go wrong.

'Don't talk to me about New York,' he says. 'You say "New York" to me I cry.' He cries about New York because he lost an apartment there. 'I mean this place? It was beautiful.' But he lost it in one of his divorces and now when he thinks of New York, he cries.

Ten, maybe fifteen years, he was in New York. 'I tell you, we did some crazy stuff. New York women, I mean...' And he shakes his head at the thought. They break your hearts, New York women. They marry you and steal your apartment in the divorce. 'The first place I had, we bought it, you know. Uptown. Man, I loved that place. But we were having a baby, you know and this was a – how do they call it? – a brownstone. You know what is a brownstone? OK, you know New York. That city, I tell you. It kills me.' And he shakes his head at another death, a death he suffers daily since the divorce. The Italians call the male orgasm 'a little death', and you can sense this in how he speaks. But – like orgasms – it is a death lived daily.

He talks about his second wife, a young American, a beautiful woman. 'But then she has this baby and she complains. The subway. The stairs. The noise. I mean, we live in the greatest city in the world and she wants silence? What is this? But so, OK, she doesn't want the stairs either, so me? I sell the house and we move to the apartment. Don't talk to me about the apartment. I tell you. I go crazy just thinking about it. The apartment was so beautiful.' And he holds his hands in that universal-but-oh-so-Italian gesture and gazes past me to a distant window of the enormous studio, while I allow him a moment's silence, out of respect for the dead.

So, OK, we don't talk about the apartment. Instead we do *il cruciverba* in last Sunday's *La Repubblica*. But I get the giggles when we do 13 down: '*Il famoso brano jazz negli cinque quarti di Dave Brubeck.*'

'Take Five?' he says. 'I wish. But that woman? She took everything.'

6 FEBRUARY 2004

## *Crazy Uncles*

'You wrote about me? My God! I must watch what I say,' says my Turinese producing colleague who has never in his life watched what he said. 'But I tell you,' he continues without looking, 'this crossword thing. You like it?' I have for some minutes been trying to explain the difference between our cryptic crosswords and the 'American' ones you find in Italian newspapers.

'Oh, my God,' he says. 'This is fun? For me this is not fun. For me this is work.' Our reading for the day came from puzzle 375 in the *Week* and I had been struggling to explain the delicate nuances of 'Pop idol after the Bill in newspaper (7).[i] 'Pop' is one of those words that simply has too many meanings for non-native speakers, especially if people start using it as an anagram indicator.

'But I tell you,' he says, 'I had an uncle. And this guy? I mean, he was mad. You know, completely crazy, like I don't know what. I mean, I like him a lot, but I was just a kid, so what do I know? So anyway. The guy's *pazzo*? You know what is *pazzo*? OK, so they lock him up. Some kind of asylum or something. And he's there for what? Thirty years, forty years. Anyway, a long time. And for forty years he writes a book which is all the crossword clues he ever did.'

I must have looked doubting.

'Serious,' he says. 'My uncle Oscar. Big book, but not published or nothing.'

As it happens the puzzle is a gem. Six clues are simply quotes from George Bush from which the solution has been omitted. 'I think we agree:—is over (3,4)'[ii] for example. Given that these are Bushisms, we can assume that the quote has a degree of nonsense to it.

My colleague approves. 'Now this I understand,' he says. 'This I can do. But these other ones? They drive you mad, no?' He laughs at a sudden thought. 'One time,' he says, 'we ask Oscar why he writes this book. And you know what he say?

'"It stops me going crazy."'

13 FEBRUARY 2004

i TABLOID; ii THE PAST

# Broad Across the Beam

The great and good were out in force on Tuesday for the opening night of Turin's revival of Jonathan Miller's remarkable production of *Le Nozze di Figaro*. I lacked both a tuxedo and a glamorous companion draped in furs, but still I managed to blend in (whom am I kidding?) with the glittering throng as we strolled through the arched walkways that surround the Piazza di Castello. No one else seemed to notice the graffiti giving a not-quite-humorous warning to Italy's former royal family: 'Savoys – if you return, we will eat you for breakfast'. Undeterred, we swept into the Teatro Regio and took our seats in its striking and dramatic auditorium.

As usual, however, my mind wasn't fully on the matter in hand. I had been glad to find a copy of the *Guardian* at the kiosk at the entrance to *via Garibaldi* on my way to the theatre and so there was the small question of the Rufus puzzle from the previous Monday. As Figaro measured the space for his wedding bed, I wrestled with the more obscure matter of his 'Miscellaneous collection of biblical characters (3,3)'.[i]

I call these clues – of which Rufus is something of a master – 'blindingly obvious'. Either you get them immediately, chuckle and move on ... or they blind you. This was one of the latter and Figaro was well into his attempts to foil the machinations of Marcellina and Dr Bartolo by the time I thought of the even more complex social relations of Job, Lot and their various offspring.

The trouble with opening nights, of course, is that people are not really there for the opera. The object is to see and be seen. Enough air was kissed in the first interval to last me a lifetime. When I opened the *Guardian* yesterday morning I wondered whether or not Logodaedalus had been there too. Like me he appeared to have noticed the 'Wide-hipped American woman in the bar (5,2,3,4)'[ii] whose views on Prime Minister Berlusconi's recent encounter with cosmetic surgery were broadcast for all and sundry to hear.

She was for it, since you ask.

27 FEBRUARY 2004

i JOB LOT; ii BROAD IN THE BEAM

## *Too Clever by Half*

My friend in Turin is not amused. 'I mean,' he says, 'what is this?' 'This' is, of course, the unusual but entertaining result in the football match between Denmark and Sweden, which ensured that Italy failed to progress to the quarter-finals of Euro 2004. All Italy knows a fix when they see one or even when they don't.

'Perhaps,' I suggest, 'it is for the best. There are more important things in life.'

'Yeah? Like what?' says my friend in a voice that suggests, actually, there aren't. 'I mean,' he continues. 'Greece are through and we are not. What is this? I mean. Have you been to Greece?' He seems to regard Greece in much the same way Anne Robinson thinks of Wales.

As it happens I had phoned him not to gloat over the football (although who would pass up the chance?) but to bemoan England's variable performances in the European Bridge Championships, where Italy have established their customary lead and where they show (at time of writing) no sign of surrendering it, despite a strong challenge from, ah, Sweden.

Another torrent of abuse follows. My friend does not regard bridge or even crosswords as the stuff of life. Diverting, yes. A pleasant way to pass an evening, perhaps. But better than sex? No.

Which brings us back, as I knew it would, to football.

Apparently it all began when Italy failed to sack their coach following their ignominious departure from the 2002 World Cup. I cast around for an easy way out of the conversation. Fortunately I have a copy of last week's puzzle from *La Repubblica* to hand, and as usual I find it has a clue for every occasion. '*Così è l'end migliore* (5)'[i] I quote, a Pollyanna to the core.

But he appears to have slammed down the phone and I find myself listening to a good long batch of dial tone. My girlfriend is not sympathetic. 'That's what you get for being hyperint,' she says.

'Hyperint?'

'Exactly so,' she agrees, '(3,6,2,4)'[ii] and she smiles as she puts the finishing touch to Paul's puzzle from Tuesday.

25 JUNE 2004

i HAPPY; ii TOO CLEVER BY HALF

---

# Getting one's Leg Over

My friend calls from Turin, which he only ever does when things have taken a turn for the worse.

'That bad?' I open pre-emptively. I'm expecting a tirade about the state of the Italian television industry.

'What do you mean bad?' he says, surprised. 'Always so negative? You should maybe see someone. I mean, a young guy like you? It's not right. No, what I got is fantastic!' And he says 'fantastic' with such emphasis that I know this can only mean he has a new woman in his life.

'You must come and visit,' he says.

'That good, huh?'

'Fantastic,' he agrees. 'I mean.'

'I'm pleased for you,' I say. 'How is …?'

But he cuts me off before I can say the name.

'Don't talk to me about her,' he says. 'I mean. What's done is done and this is done. It's over. I'm sorry, OK? Maybe I did wrong, I don't know. Who knows what's wrong these days? I mean, you can invade a country, kill some children, but you can't make love? But, so, maybe I was a little bit wrong. Maybe I did things in the wrong order. Anyway, there's no going back. Finished.' And, with that verbal dexterity I so admire, he says 'finished' in seven or eight other languages.

'So it's over?' I ask. No one can accuse me of being slow.

'So English,' he says. 'Always looking back. *That* may be over but *this* is only just beginning. We think maybe we'll buy a place together. Nothing fancy. Maybe by the lakes. Bit of land, view of the water. Someplace we can make beautiful. You ever fall in love, you'll know what I mean. So what are you doing?'

I am, of course, doing the Cyclops puzzle in *Private Eye*. I'm wondering whether to admit this when I realize the answer to a clue I've been puzzling over for the past few minutes: 'It's said you might get your leg over this with a certain elegance (5)'.[i]

Which my friend has, in abundance.

1 OCTOBER 2004

i STYLE

---

## *A Burning Desire*

Our eyes meet across a crowded room ... and then like everyone else in that hotbed of celibacy we call the British Library, we look away.

But later at the issuing desk there is a stand-off when the French researcher and I request the same book on Hugh Latimer. My interest is his 'sermons on the cards', which he delivered in 1529 and which are thought to be the earliest written reference to 'trumps' as used in card games; she is writing about methods used to kill heretics. 1200–1800. Or possibly 1300–1900. My French is less than adequate for the task. I know Latimer was burned at the stake in Oxford, but I have only recently heard of the parting gift from his brother, or (by some accounts), Ridley's brother – bags of gunpowder, which he hung about the condemned men's necks, the better to speed their going.

She appears later in the coffee shop where I am busy with the *Telegraph* crossword.

There is some kind of contretemps at the counter. Voices are raised, together with objections. 'Ridiculous,' she says, with that oh-so-French contempt. 'In 1553 it cost less to burn Latimer and Ridley than this cup of so-called hot chocolate cost me today?' From a flurry of papers she recovers a note. 'Here, look. Three loads of wood, twelve shillings. Furze, three and fourpence. Carriage for wood, two shillings. A post, one and fourpence. Two chains, three and fourpence. Two staples, sixpence. Four labourers, two and eight. Total, One pound, five shillings and twopence.' She looks at her hot chocolate. 'And for this I must pay two pounds? Ridiculous.'

Leaving moral considerations aside (and where else is one to leave them?) I had to agree that the good Queen Mary got excellent value for her money. The hot chocolate is a more dubious bargain.

'Why burn?' I ask. 'Why not hang?'

'Spectacle,' she replies. 'They did it for show.'

But my eyes stray back to Wednesday's crossword. 'Perhaps they had "A burning desire (9)"?'[i] I murmur.

The French researcher gives every impression of being unimpressed.

8 OCTOBER 2004

i PYROMANIA

# *Amour-propre*

At the British Library I am diligently drinking coffee and reading what is possibly the finest piece of reporting I have seen all year. 'A wallaby,' the *Guardian* told us on Wednesday, 'reported to be on the loose in Cardiff is now thought to be an injured fox.'

Well, indeed. One looked for more but there was none. That was it, the entire story in a single, elegantly constructed sentence. No more need be said. One could imagine other stories given the same treatment. Boris Johnson reported to be a lovable maverick is now thought to be a threat to all this nation holds dear. Tony Blair reported to be honest…well, you fill in the rest.

My musings are disturbed by a flurry of perfume and books. My friend, the French researcher, scatters herself on the chair opposite. 'For you English,' she rails, 'it is so clever to say one thing and mean another?' Again, this says it all. Over the course of several coffee breaks I have become familiar with the pattern, if not the detail, of her affair with an officer of one of 'the services', though I have yet to discover which one.

'Again?' I ask.

She nods. 'It is no good. Every time I think we have – how do you say, the understanding? – I find we do not.'

'Things change,' I suggest, diplomatically. 'Especially if you're in the…?'

But she ignores my cue and for want of anything else to say I mention that in crosswords, of course, the point of the exercise for the setters is to say what they mean while at the same time there is no requirement at all that they should mean what they say. By way of illustration we do the two clues forming the main axis of the Janus puzzle from a couple of weeks ago. In the red corner we have this clue: 'Trophy girls tricked into serious predicament (5,6)'.[i] And in the blue corner: 'Love affair involving proper self-respect (5-6)'.[ii]

I'm sure there's a lesson in there somewhere.

22 OCTOBER 2004

i SORRY PLIGHT; ii AMOUR-PROPRE

---

## *Torquemada*

My Italian friend is slightly tipsy. 'So who are these people anyway? I mean. Old? Young? They fall in love or what?' He believes that to be human is to fall in love, and possibly vice versa. The 'people' he has in mind are crossword setters. 'I mean, they have lives?'

Well, who's to say? But by way of illustration I draw his attention to the newly republished collection of poems translated by E. Powys Mathers. Mathers is better known to crossword solvers as Torquemada, but when not setting puzzles for the *Observer* – it was he who established the tradition of the 'difficult' puzzle, continued later by Ximenes and now by Azed – Mathers was a playwright, critic and bon viveur of the sort my friend would approve. In his introduction to the beautiful new edition of *Black Marigolds & Coloured Stars* (Anvil Press, £7.95), Tony Harrison describes Mathers as an 'erotic aesthete, cocktail-shaking

Chinese-American, honorary Arab nomad, bhang-chewer, Turkish bisexual' and concludes that he 'was a true if minor poet whose assimilation of Eastern modes should rank with Arthur Waley or Ezra Pound, and whose name and achievement should be better known than they are.'

He was also, as Harrison says, a 'tormenting puzzle-setter'. Mathers died in 1939. Writing the foreword to a collection of his '112 Best Crossword Puzzles', published first in 1942, his wife Rosamund touches on that most curious quality of puzzles – that through them solvers feel they come to 'know' the setter. She quotes one solver who wrote to mourn his passing. 'It is not merely their tortuous ingenuity that made his puzzles unique – he had no monopoly of tortuousness or ingenuity – it was that they reflected at so many angles the character, knowledge and humanity of their author.'

My Italian friend is impressed. 'I mean,' he says, putting aside the puzzle collection and picking up the volume of poems. 'These are love poems?'

'They are.'

He pauses. 'You know what? I take this book. I mean, if I buy the book, maybe I will meet someone to give it to?'

5 NOVEMBER 2004

## Happy Families

The United States has asserted its right to strike in advance at its enemies, and in keeping with these pre-emptive times, I apologize in advance. It doesn't matter what for. This is a generic, all embracing, one size fits all apology, and no less heartfelt for all that.

And besides, it's not my fault. For had not the French researcher inquired why it is that I no longer mention her in my despatches from my desk at the British Library, and had not my Italian friend arrived unannounced and unaccompanied (a disturbing combination which usually means he is in want of a wife, and not necessarily his own either) then neither of them would have been invited to brave the gales and tramp with us on a wet and windy afternoon across the gloomy midwinter curves of Hampstead Heath.

But they did and we did and I'm sorry.

For I am certain that into each life some rain must fall. But the fact remains that after an hour or so of this hellish delight we settled in at Kenwood for a ritual coffee and crossword. Well – I did, while acknowledging the sad fact that I find it hard to imagine coffee without one, much as some smokers cannot have a drink without reaching for a cigarette. My Italian friend and the French researcher, who until that point had shown no real interest in each other, laughed, shared a slice of chocolate fudge cake, discovered a mutual interest in pre-Raphaelite painting and were soon suggesting that perhaps it was not necessary for them to walk all the way back across the Heath to our house and that really it would be better all round if they simply made their way to the Spaniards Road, from where they were sure it would be possible to share a cab to some, ah, mutually convenient point.

Which left my girlfriend and me looking at the Everyman puzzle in the *Observer* and wondering whether they would soon be playing the 'Card game that's pleased generations (5,8)'?[i] My girlfriend was more optimistic. 'Not everything must be dark and dreary,' she said, as a shaft of light broke through the threatening clouds.

14 JANUARY 2005

i HAPPY FAMILIES

---

## *Breakfast in Belsize Park*

It is not so much the mention of Holly Golightly that gets the attention of my Italian friend, as the reminiscences of the narrator of *Breakfast at Tiffany's* who, in the second sentence of the novel mentions 'an old brownstone in the east seventies where ...'

'Please,' says my friend. 'Please no brownstones, OK. I am a little hurt here, OK?' And he beats his chest lest I misread the nature of his pain. Followers of this column may remember that some years ago, while working as a television producer in New York, my friend lost a brownstone in the course of one of his divorces.*

'I mean, not lost, you know? I know where it is, but...' He shakes his head and anyway he is more concerned to understand what he thinks of as the curious behaviour of the French researcher who, having agreed to share a taxi with him, kissed him on the cheek, alighted at Belsize Park and promised to call.

Which, as of Wednesday, she had not done.

'I mean,' he said disconsolately, but he couldn't find any words to express his dismay. 'What is this?'

Well, actually it was the Enigmatist puzzle from last Saturday, the theme of which was Truman Capote's wonderful novel, and which had been causing me a certain amount of emotional and intellectual – what's the word? – grief.

'Exactly!' said my friend. 'That's exactly it. Grief. This woman, she is grief.'

Which seemed to me to be a little harsh, for while Holly may be flawed, there is no doubt that she represents a yearning in all of us, and I cannot remember except with a pang her restless travelling in search of a home, or at least a place where she could 'feel at home'.

'What are you saying?' asks my friend, but I am lost to his emotional woes. 'This type shoots back (5),'[i] I mutter. And it's only later that I realize he thinks I am talking about the French researcher who, by her own admission, bears a faint resemblance to Audrey Hepburn.

* See p. 41–2.

* See p. 41–2.

21 JANUARY 2005
i SERIF

## Putting one's Foot in It

Many thanks to all those who wrote in with endings for Araucaria's limerick and even more thanks for those who tactfully didn't point out I had misquoted the first two lines. An International Committee was set up to decide the winner and after extensive deliberation my mum decided that Stephanie Rybak gets the box of Divine Fairtrade chocolate for this effort:

There was a tragedian from Gwelo
Who wrote a Zimbabwean Othello.
Othello was white,
The actors were tight
And the set a Harare bordello.

My girlfriend, needless to say, did not agree, but she is forbidden from saying so under the terms of an elaborate truce recently agreed between ourselves that in matters of this column I am always right. She, therefore, is invariably wrong, although I do concede that she was prescient (which is not the same as being right) to suggest that the French researcher would be better off entering a pit of vipers than going on a second date with 'that short one from Turin, the one with the moustache' or, (as I think of him), my Italian friend.

Things started badly, and got worse. His joke about the state of French rugby foundered on the rocks of her rugby-loving father's recent death. He then stepped out of the cab to open the door for her, only to find himself knee deep in slush. She, perhaps from remorse, cackled loudly and remarked that it was lucky he wasn't any shorter. 'For whom?' he inquired, as she snapped her boot heel in a storm drain.

Which all goes to show, as Pasquale pointed out on Tuesday, that 'Nowadays, people of both sexes may put their foot in it (7,3)'.[i]

25 FEBRUARY 2005

i TROUSER LEG

# A Plea for Inconstancy

'Love,' said A.P. Wavell, 'is almost as universal an experience as death, with the advantage from a poet's point of view that it is possible to write of it from personal experience.' He was writing in one of the prefaces to the different sections of his beautiful anthology, *Other Men's Flowers*. I am delighted to find that it is still in print, more than sixty years after it was first published.

There are two organizing principles behind the anthology. The first is that they are all poems the late Field Marshall could recite by heart. 'Though his phenomenal memory was well known to his friends, others may query this statement, but it is true and accounts for the omission of works he admired but did not remember,' it says in the introduction to the edition I have (Penguin, 1960). The second is a number of headings under which the poems are collected: 'Music, Mystery, and Magic', 'Good Fighting', 'The Call of the Wild' and so on.

Wavell's comments on love come in his introduction to the section entitled 'Love and All That' and he goes on, rather disarmingly, to wonder whether 'a poet, or any man' (he was a child of his time!) should have one love or many?

Well, who's to say? Shelley, in 'Epipsychidion', is in no doubt as to the answer and as Wavell notes, many poets conclude that 'a singleton heart is seldom a satisfactory holding'. Even Browning, the most faithful of lovers, puts in 'a disarming plea for inconstancy'. 'Ah, but the fresher faces,' he wrote, and we all know what he means.

I once wrote that 'discovering Araucaria was like falling in love' and it was true. The same giddy anticipation of delight. The same frustration. The occasional suspicion that he doesn't take you seriously. After all, it was he who suggested that 'First love is indigo (4)'.[i] Which may be why Wavell wondered whether the old music-hall song had a point:

If you can't be true to one or two
You're much better off with three...

12 AUGUST 2005

i ANIL

---

# RELATIVE VALUES

# Araucaria at Top Table

One of the myths of crosswords is that doing them is a solitary pastime, both for the setters and the solvers. In my experience the opposite is true and I prefer to think of them as an on-going conversation about our language and our times. It may be fragmented, inconsequential and incomplete – but it is a conversation nonetheless. Most solvers have a crossword-companion, a person they turn to first to share clues and compare solutions.

As it happens my crossword companion is also my girlfriend, except that recently she has gone on a series of wildcat strikes.

'It's not fun any more,' she said on Tuesday after I had made the mistake of solving a clue too quickly. 'I preferred it when you were useless.' The implied compliment notwithstanding, this seemed unnecessarily harsh.

'When was that?' I asked.

'1962 onwards…'

It was a conversation, I decided, best left unfinished.

For others their first crossword companion is a parent. This week I was e-mailed by one *Guardian* solver who had posted a message about his father on this newspaper's crossword chat room.

They loved to do the prize puzzle together and once even won the prize. But a few weeks ago that changed for ever.

One Sunday evening with the Taupi puzzle not yet complete, the solver's father was suddenly taken ill. He died a day later. 'Life and crosswords will never be the same without Dad,' my correspondent writes. 'I find it strange on a weekend not to be able to pick up the phone and see how he's doing on the puzzle.' His greatest memory of his father, he continues, was his wedding at which his father, who was a brilliant calligrapher, had written all the place cards and table name cards, 'the tables being named after crossword compilers. He (and I) were proud to be sitting at the top table: Araucaria.'

It's a beautiful tribute – to a setter and a solver – even though we learn about it in the context of what will always be an unfinished conversation between a father and his son.

7 NOVEMBER 2003

## *Aloof Loofahs*

You can imagine the scene. The windows are steamed up. The bath is hot. The bubble bath has bubbled nicely. My son and daughter are in the bath and so far they have neither spilled water on the floor nor got soap in their eyes. My son gives himself a moustache, while my daughter giggles and puts a wet 'X' on his forehead. My girlfriend is downstairs doing the crossword puzzle. All is well with our world.

It cannot possibly last.

'Where's the loofah?' says my son. It's a word that appeals to eight-year-old boys. I look around, but there is no sign of it. I search behind the toilet and in the basin cupboard. No loofah.

I turn out the laundry basket and reach behind the bookshelves on the landing. Nothing.

'I'll scrub you,' says my daughter helpfully and she slaps a dollop of bubbles on his head. It is not long therefore before the first piece of soap makes contact with the first eye and the first yell pierces the blue of eve. A splash of water sails over the edge of the bath.

It is time for Supermum. 'Yo!' I yell, (forgive me; this is a verbatim transcript) 'Have you see the loofah?'

'Sure,' she says absently. '22 across. I got it straight away.' And because she is under the impression that I have time on my hands, she reads out the clue from Shed's puzzle last Wednesday: '"Sponge for dessert sent back with sigh of relief (6)".'[i]

'Really?' I ask.

'Really. Why?'

Well, because there had been a 'loofah' clue – 'Reserved a scrubber with no expression of joy (5)'[ii] – in last Saturday's puzzle, and you don't get many of those. Like London buses, they all come at once.

Another yell draws me upstairs, but by the time I get there my son has mysteriously found the loofah and my daughter has ceased to play tic-tac-toe on his forehead. She starts to wash her hair, which causes me to sigh with relief, while my son lies back in the water wearing a curious expression of joy.

Aaahh.

21 November 2003

i LOOFAH; ii ALOOF

# Everything is about Something Else

A letter arrives from a crossword fan to share a saying that sustains him both in his professional life and when he is attempting crosswords. He attributes it to a former head of UNESCO who wanted people to think before they came to him. And so he put a note up on his door. 'Everything,' it read, 'is about something else.'

My girlfriend was not interested in the whimsy of international bureaucrats. She has been through a crossword renaissance of late and tends to hog the *Guardian* over the breakfast table. I make do with more esoteric fry.

'You should try this,' I said, pulling, in the manner of a magician, a copy of Alamet's Christmas special from the *Morning Star*. In what must surely be the setter's only mention in that esteemed organ, one reader praised Alamet saying that 'in comparison, Araucaria's Christmas special was slim pickings.'

She tried it. For about twenty seconds.

'Uh, uh,' she concluded. 'Any puzzle where I have to read the preamble more than three times isn't worth it.'

Except it was, because buried inside the puzzle with the overwrought preamble were some fun clues. But to do them you had to accept that each clue was actually two clues for two solutions (to be filled in identical grids) and that all four- and five-letter solutions in the first grid 'shared a common theme and those parts of the clues did not have definitions'.

For example? 'Assumed second murder is committed without the first sign of remorse if a European has not married girl by the end of June, selected from those with a birthday between two dates (8; 3,5)'.[i]

Well, this clue makes a kind of sense, doesn't it?

'No,' said my girlfriend.

'And it's fun,' I suggested.

'I'll stick with slim pickings,' she replied.

'You're "far from satisfied with a mouthful? (3,2,2,3,4,5)"'[ii] I retorted, but only because I was trying to be clever and had done one down in yesterday's Araucaria.

'Make the packed lunches,' she said, but what she really meant was 'Hands off, that puzzle's mine.'

10 JANUARY 2004

i SURMISED, AGE RANGE; ii FED UP TO THE BACK TEETH

---

## *As they Grow Up they Grow Down*

Paul Merton's wonderful ability to keep a gag running, especially on *Have I Got News for You*, occasionally gets him into trouble. I remember a few seasons back – this was still the Angus Deayton era – when he answered a question some time after it was asked, for which Deayton duly mocked him.

'That was an earlier question,' he said.

'I know. I'm psychic,' Merton replied unperturbed. 'But my timing's off.'

Janus' timing – or that of the crossword editor – was similarly off yesterday: 'Naughty teaser urges seasonal treats (6, 4)'.[i] But for a seasonal treat on Sunday we headed for Hyde Park and the rollerblading area beside the Serpentine.

We arrived early, before the afternoon crowds of dancers and racers. Even so it represents something of an obstacle race. If the ducks don't get you, the unleashed dogs will. My son eschews the frivolity of rollerblading in favour of skateboarding, which means that his sister and I get to tow him along while he helpfully yells things like 'faster' and 'I never noticed before how big your bum is'. At the eastern end of the tarmac there is a slight incline and it is possible to pick up a decent speed on the return leg.

Sailing thus in formation we had just reached the 'point of no return' ('Rubicon is ace (5,2,2,6)' according to Paul on Tuesday) – which is to say the point at which my son's confident chants change to a whispered 'not so fast' – when a duck chose to walk in front of us.

You can imagine what ensued. All I will report is that no animals except me were hurt in the making of this scene. I landed on the ground. My children landed on me. And the duck went on its merry way.

'Thanks,' said my daughter.

'Why couldn't you land on the duck?' I asked.

'It wouldn't have been as soft,' she replied.

At which point my girlfriend diplomatically intervened. '"As it grows up it grows down (8)",'[ii] she said, quoting from a puzzle last week in the *Glasgow Herald*.

16 APRIL 2004

i EASTER EGGS; ii DUCKLING

## *To Err is Human*

My friend was living up to her crossword clue ('Woman is a pain in both sides (6)'[i]) by declining to let me thrash her at tennis. Some years ago I used to beat her with relative ease, but that was before she emigrated to South Africa where they take winning more seriously. From time to time she returns to London, fitter, browner and less appeasing than before, and we play. And so for an hour or so on Wednesday I found myself chasing the distant shadows of her forehand drives down the line.

It's like that with crosswords sometimes. Solutions that should be – or perhaps once were – simple and obvious elude us, while others seem to hover around the edges of our consciousness, frustratingly close, impossibly distant.

Sitting in the coffee shop in Muswell Hill after the game, it was not, for example, too difficult for us to guess **TERRITORY** was the solution to this clue in that morning's Pasquale: 'What is human but loveless – one politician establishing dominion (9)', but it took a while to work out why.

I suppose it depended on what came to mind when you read the words 'to be human'. To be human is to … what? According to the great god Google, to be human is (in the order presented) 'to live', 'to feel', 'to love', 'to seek understanding', 'to be auto-homo-hetero-erotic' (and that's from a learned tome published by Harvard Square Library, so it must be true), 'to be aware of our separation' and so on. Take the 'o' of 'loveless' out of any of those and you're no closer to working out why we had the right answer. At least it was clear that 'one politician' gave us 'ITORY'. But 'TERR'?

So we talked about the tennis. There was one particular moment in the game, a decisive moment even, when I might have swayed things my way by playing softly instead of hitting the smash that landed in the back fence.

'I always make that mistake,' I said.

'To err is human,' she replied, but even then I couldn't see it.

28 May 2004

i RACHEL

---

## Boy Bands

My daughter (I won't say which one, for fear of retribution) currently has something of a crush on a particular member of a boy band (sorry, highly credible and authentic rock group) and spends much of her time perusing the popular press and the web in order that she might know where and when this band is performing or (better still) merely appearing in public. She is willing then to travel vast distances for a glimpse of the boys (sorry, artists) and the blond one in particular. My nine-year-old son, by contrast, is a fan of the Red Hot Chili Peppers and goes around singing with what I can only hope is irony or blissful ignorance of 'Californication' and the like.

I find I am curiously sympathetic to my daughter, if only because there was a time in my life when I had very deep and meaningful close personal relationships with both Olivia

Newton John and the 'dark one' from Abba. So it was that when I was in Memphis recently I could not pass up the opportunity to drive the forty miles or so to the casinos of Tunica where I secured at vast expense a ticket to see Olivia (as I thought of her) perform 'live on stage'.

Sadly, however, I have never seen Abba 'live on stage' but I live in hope that they will one day reunite for the mother of all middle-aged parties in Hyde Park. I had always assumed their name to be derived from the initials of the performers' names. So I suspect did they. It took Gordius on Tuesday ('Biblical father of pop (4)'[i] to show me that the word is much older than that and appears three times in the New Testament. It essentially means father, but is a 'deeper' concept and expresses 'the peculiar tenderness, familiarity, and confidence of the love between parent and child', though probably not between adolescent and world-class pop act.

Come to think of it, Gordius was on a bit of a roll: 'Song about issue of Atlas (7)'[ii] anyone?

6 APRIL 2005

i ABBA; ii CALYPSO

## *The Cake under the Cherry*

All marriages involve compromise (you can quote me on this) but some compromises are more compromising than others. Ask Rod Liddle for details. I mention this only because my girlfriend and I had the great pleasure of attending a party last week at which two friends celebrated thirty years of unwedded bliss by getting married. Perhaps there's a fashion for it; this was the third such event to which we had been invited in as many months. And so in that curiously modern way their children had done the organizing and all that was required was for our friends to enjoy their day.

I found myself in conversation with an occasional reader of these columns. 'You have to write about me,' she said, 'because I did it. Last Saturday. Honest.' She was a little breathless just at the thought of it. 'Araucaria's prize puzzle, without any help, on my own, I solved a clue.'

'Actually it's quite apposite,' she added, lest I fail to work that out for myself.

I had done the puzzle during the rain intervals in the Wimbledon men's final and was pretty sure I knew what was coming. '"Woman's right, always (4)",'[i] she quoted. But the solution had not yet been published and she had a moment of doubt about her answer. I hastened to reassure her that the woman is right, always.

'Perhaps we should tell him?' she said, meaning the groom.

'After thirty years, he probably knows.'

We looked over to where the couple were dancing. The music had slowed and they were in a fingertip embrace, moving easily apart to allow the flow of other dancers, yet somehow always in touch. 'Except nobody leads anymore,' the occasional reader said continuing an otherwise unspoken thought. 'Perhaps that's why it works.'

In any case it was a delightful party; the rain held off, the bride was radiant and the fireworks reflected brightly in the still waters of the midnight lake.

It was, agreed the groom's mother, the cake under the cherry.

'I'm the cherry,' said her grandson as he ran to organize the champagne.

16 JULY 2004

## *Kilimanjaro (1)*

Before travelling to the furthest reaches of Siberia, my daughter and I are attempting to climb Mount Kilimanjaro. The summit is at 5,895 metres above sea level and the tour company are keen to make the final agony – sorry, ascent – as memorable as possible. They're also keen to get you back down. For this reason the final climb – this is after four days' hiking – begins at midnight. You scramble up the last 800 metres by the light of the full moon and the theory is that you reach the summit just in time to watch the sun rise somewhere over the Indian Ocean.

In preparation for this I have been forced to eschew crosswords in favour of more strenuous forms of exercise. I have, for example, discovered that the exit spiral at our local tube station has 116 steps. Assuming each step is 23 centimetres high (he said, reaching for his calculator) if I climb the steps a mere 222 times, I will have climbed the height of Kilimanjaro. Allowing for altitude sickness I should...

Sadly the presiding officer at the tube station was not in the mood to allow for altitude sickness. We were barely into our twelfth ascent before he wished to know in no uncertain terms what was all this here?

I replied that all this here was an honourable attempt to use local resources in order to prepare to climb the world's highest freestanding mountain, but it cut no mustard with our man. 'You'll have to buy a ticket,' he said.

Which we did. By the eighteenth ascent I was knackered. By twenty-five it was all over. And at thirty I gave up. I should have known; Quixote in the *Independent on Sunday* had already warned that 'Second highest peak is the most demanding (8)'.[i]

I think I'll stick to crosswords. At least I can sometimes finish them.

30 JULY 2004

i SEVEREST

# *Lovely – and vague*

'You, who're so good with words, and at keeping things vague…' Joan Baez may use it as an accusation in *Diamonds and Rust*, her love/hate tribute to Bob Dylan, but I have always thought vagueness a much underrated quality. Of course in matters of love one always wants the other half to be unequivocal. 'Do you love me?' is not the sort of question that allows for much prevarication.

As all who have tried it will know.

But in art or politics I find a little vagueness goes a long way. It was John Locke, writing in 1690, who first used the word in its modern sense of 'not precise or exact in meaning', although he too was against it. 'Vague and insignificant forms of speech, and abuse of language, have so long passed for mysteries of science…' he complained. A few years later Locke used it again in the sense of 'indefinite or indistinct'. He had no time for *vague* ideas. But I like the word and its wandering roots just as I like the soft edges of great distances and just as I prefer the intangible scent of victory to the fact.

The word derives, of course, from the Latin *vagus*, meaning wandering, and as such is a cousin of those other words for the feckless and dissident: vagary and vagrant. And you have only to browse in the new *Chambers Thesaurus* to get the sense of possibility in the word: hazy, misty, nebulous, amorphous…

Which brings me to my girlfriend.

As a general rule my girlfriend is a practical person. Ask her a straight question and she will give you a straight answer. Mostly.

The night in question was balmy. A gentle breeze plucked the neighbourhood trees. Quiet filled the air and the edges of the city blurred in gentle light. So I asked, foolishly, not whether she loved me, but how much.

On which question she remained, as Falcon put it in that morning's *Financial Times*, 'Lovely and vague (6)'.[i] For, as Mark Antony told Cleopatra, 'there's beggary in the love that can be reckon'd'.

6 August 2004

i DREAMY

# Kilimanjaro (2)

What would you pay for a crossword? Until recently I would have said 'not much' – but put to the test, I found the answer is 'a ridiculous amount'. Desperate Times, it seems, require Desperate Measures.

Even as we descended Mount Kilimanjaro last week the engine of an East African Safari Air (EASA) Boeing 767-300 caught fire, forcing the pilot to make an emergency landing at Rome's Leonardo da Vinci Airport. None of the 165 passengers or ten crew members was injured and the fire was quickly extinguished by a built-in mechanism on the aeroplane. But EASA is not a large airline and the withdrawal of 50 per cent of its international fleet meant that passengers were left flightless at a series of airports in Kenya and Tanzania.

Including Kilimanjaro International. My daughter, who had a book and an unlimited coke-and-crisps budget, was reasonably content, but as the hours passed I found myself pacing the departures lounge with increasing frustration. At the rate this was going we wouldn't be able to join the rest of the family for another twenty-four hours.

'Go find a crossword,' said my daughter. 'There's an internet café.'

There is? There was! Up some stairs, around a corner, down a passage and there was a computer. And for only $1 per minute I could download anything I liked. The connection was slow and there was no printer, but I found Paul's prize puzzle 22,203, drew the grid by hand and wrote out all the clues. It took twenty-three minutes, making it by some distance my most expensive crossword ever.

But these were desperate times and JRO (as we old lags know it) is not an airport where time passes quickly.

It was, in fact, twenty-eight hours before EASA managed to get us to our destination, a mere fifty minutes' flying time away. We found the others drinking coconut juice by the pool.

"'Entury? (4,4,2,3)",'[i] said my girlfriend, who had got the paper from another traveller, but it took the rest of the day for me to work out what on earth she and Paul meant by this.

16 AUGUST 2004

i LONG TIME NO SEE

## *Viagra for the* Eminence Grise

A Bunthorne puzzle, I find, usually requires a long summer's or long winter's evening. He is simply not a setter for the equinoxes. His prize puzzle last month was a case in point and the beautiful evening, marred only by thunder and torrential rain, seemed to me to be the perfect time to settle in quietly for the long haul.

My girlfriend was in good form, or perhaps her mind was elsewhere. In any case it took her only a moment to spot that the solution to 'Hardy, failed poet? Not lacking love (6)'[i] was not a reference to the creator of so many forlorn-but-fictional lovers. This was good because it gave her the required solution to complete another clue: 'Sylvia Grahame's part in making one [potent] (6)'.[ii]

'I wonder what he was thinking about?' she asked absently. It was hard to be fully focused when the heavens threatened at any moment to rupture completely and sweep us all away in the long forgotten Fleet River. 'I mean, is this like a theme or a code?' Like many solvers my girlfriend harbours dark suspicions that puzzles contain secret messages. She hasn't forgotten the story of the *Telegraph* puzzles from 1944 that were suspected of revealing the D-Day plans to the enemy because they contained words like 'mulberry', 'Omaha' and 'overlord'.

'I'm sure it is just coincidence,' I murmured. The west wind battered the conservatory with unremitting delight and I wondered briefly whether I should go and check our house insurance before the roof took off for warmer climes. The television pictures of Florida in the aftermath of Hurricane Charley were all too fresh in my mind.

'I mean, what's this?' my girlfriend asked. '"Père Joseph's *crise en ménage* when one makes way for a revolution (8,5)"?'[iii] It took a while to find the anagram hidden in there. 'Oh for heaven's sake,' she said when she got it, 'perhaps the whole sodding puzzle is about you.'

'Except for the "eminence" part,' said my daughter who listens in more than she should.

3 SEPTEMBER 2004

i POTENT; ii VIAGRA; iii EMINENCE GRISE

---

# Metallic Irony

Contrary to popular opinion many crossword solvers live whole-some and useful lives, generating wealth, rescuing cats, robbing banks and so on. Some go so far as to have ambitions or even careers and I once met one who was said to have every intention of winning a Nobel Prize for Physics.

For the rest of us, however, there are crossword chat rooms on the Internet in which it is possible to while away the long winter evenings debating the nature of the perfect crossword clue. Or the imperfect nature of other people's crossword clues. In which case you may prefer to pop to your local literary café (this may be a north-London phenomenon; in my neck of the woods we have not one but two of these strange beasts) where seated in the corner there will be a gentleperson of leisure, drinking coffee, enjoying a last roll-up before it becomes a hanging offence, and doing the crossword.

This being a literary café, the chances are his paper of choice will be the *Guardian* or the *Independent*, but occasionally you may have the rare treat of finding a former city bigwig doing the puzzle in the *FT*. In which case he will be – all right, I'll come clean – he *was* frustrated by Wednesday's puzzle by Cinephile in which there appeared no fewer than thirteen of the Irish Republic's twenty-six counties. Mostly undefined, of course. Cinephile is better known in the *Guardian* as Araucaria and the preamble had a familiar ring to it: 'Solutions to asterisked clues are all of a kind and usually have no further definition'. But it was in the gaps between the asterisks that the gems were to be found. Even with all the checked letters my new companion was unable to see through the definition in this clue: 'Irony, perhaps, unbelievable after setter's in charge (8)'.[i]

I couldn't see it either, and it was left to my girlfriend to solve it that evening. 'The irony,' she said, 'is in the definition because the definition is in the irony.'

I think she meant to be helpful.

19 NOVEMBER 2004

i METALLIC

## Diary of a Nobody

'You're getting fat,' said my daughter this week, an observation which made up in truth what it lacked in tact. I mention this only because, as a self-confessed member of the confessional school of journalism, I feel I owe it to Mr Charles Pooter of The Laurels, Brickfield Terrace, Holloway to be as frank as possible in these columns. It was Mr Pooter who set the standard – and gave the *apologia pro vita sua* – for the rest of us.

'Why,' he says in the introduction to his *Diary of a Nobody*, 'should I not publish my diary? I have often seen reminiscences of people I have never even heard of, and I fail to see – because I do not happen to be a 'Somebody' – why my diary should not be interesting. My only regret is that I did not commence it when I was a youth.'

Well, indeed. We should all reminisce more in these dislocating times. It is worth mentioning though that George Grossmith, who wrote the *Diary* with his brother Weedon, was by any standards a 'somebody' who took leading roles in many of Gilbert and Sullivan's operettas, and collaborated with Gilbert in writing others. The *Diary* appeared originally as a column of light relief in *Punch*, but in 1892 they decided to publish it as a novel and it has been in print ever since.

I was driven to reread it this week when I came across this clue by Virgilius in Monday's *Independent*: 'Literary diarist's criticism of wine (6)'.[i] But the book is too good to put down, and what should have been a brief foray to the bookshelves turned into a few hours of lost delight as, mince pies close to hand, I followed Mr Pooter and the long-suffering Carrie while they dealt with all that life and the dreadful Lupin could throw at them.

Eventually I had to stop reading and go to play some tennis. While the clue's criticism may be true of some wines, sadly the same cannot be said of me.

Well, not in both senses.

17 DECEMBER 2004

i NOBODY

# *A Load of Bull*

Blessed as I was from childhood with the looks and demeanour of an old man, I find I am untroubled by the passage of time and its attendant ravages. Age cannot wither me, for I am already withered, but my girlfriend, being a person of considerable beauty and charm, regards the advancing years with the sort of baleful glare that vultures reserve for the living. And so I was not surprised this week to find that we were celebrating her thirty-seventh birthday for the sixth (or was it seventh?) consecutive year.

This was also the week in which my daughter turned fourteen, which (as you'll know if you spend too much time reading the *Guardian*) is a challenging time for all concerned. The issue of the week (apparently when they turn fifteen the issues come daily, but for the moment they are only weekly) concerns piercing, which I regard as a form of self-mutilation that should be strongly discouraged. My daughter naturally regards it as an important matter of civil liberty and the right to choose (no, not *that* right) and my girlfriend thinks it is something we could perhaps discuss in a rational and pleasant manner to the mutual satisfaction of all.

And we're only talking about her ears.

The rational and pleasant conversation is not going my daughter's way, not even when I quote my favourite line from Munro Leaf's incomparable book, *Ferdinand the Bull*. 'Sometimes his mother, who was a cow, worried about him.' I mean it by way of explanation, but my daughter is not impressed. 'Don't bully me with your love,' she says.

Which made it that much easier to do Bunthorne on Wednesday: 'Ferdinand sleeps with cows (9)',[i] but which left the question of the ears unresolved.

1 APRIL 2005

i BULLDOZES

---

# *Everyone a Winner*

My son is developing a disturbing taste for riddles. More encouragingly he is starting to like his rugby. This is because he is now old enough legitimately to thump (sorry, tackle) opposing players. He doesn't have to use tags like the under-nines any more.

'Guess what?' he said when I called home last Sunday.

'What?'

'You know two days before next Tuesday...?' (I'm embarrassed to say it took me a long moment to work out what this meant.)

'Ye-es?'

'Well, two days before next Tuesday I won a medal.'

There is a pause. (Told you it was embarrassing.)

'You mean today?'

'Nice one, Dad.'

He's very excited and so am I. His team have come first in a tournament involving nine other clubs. I congratulate him on his success. He tells me about the time eight opposing players tried to tackle him. He recounts the details of both tries he scored, but reserves his greatest praise for Hughie, who scored nine.

'Why did you phone?' he asks.

Well, actually it's because it is my tennis club's first tournament of the season and my partner Jane and I have, through no fault of our own, got through to the final. We will have to stay and play one more match, which means I will be late for dinner. But I don't want to spoil his moment.

'Just tell Mum I will be late,' I say.

There are noises off before he comes back on the line.

'She says you're already late,' he says.

I arrive home (very) late, but victorious (but that's another story) to find my son looking like a shop-soiled Johnny Wilkinson. He has his medal and a black eye for his pains. He is marginally more proud of the eye.

For, as Paul said yesterday, it's a 'Game not to cry over (6)'.[i]

15 APRIL 2005

i BOSTON

---

# *A Sobering Tale*

The white smoke in my life this week came not from the papal conclave, but from the slightly drunk man at the bar with whom I had foolishly started a discussion on my Scottish roots.

'Scotland,' he said firmly, 'is our Mexico.'

'It is?'

'You mark my words,' he said and then he closed his eyes for several minutes leaving me no wiser as to what, if anything, this might mean.

It's my fault. I mentioned that I had been digging around in my family's collective memory, which is how I know that in 1691 James Balfour was expelled from the United Presbytery for the sin of adultery. And my great-grandfather George was an elder of the Kirk in Hawick towards the end of the nineteenth century. But he became involved in an acrimonious battle over funding for the roof of the church, which was in a state of disrepair and through which the winter rains were prone to flow in copious volumes. A wealthy but abstemious benefactor offered to pay for the repairs and it was held to be an excellent thing when he imposed only one condition – that non-alcoholic wine should be used for communion. For George this was unthinkable, an affront to the dignity of every drinking man and (so his namesake, my uncle George, recounts gleefully) he opposed the move saying that it was better, so to speak, to be wet than dry. After some weeks of ever more high-flown and impassioned oratory the matter was put to the vote. The hard-headed realists won overwhelmingly, and George had little option but to resign.

No wonder my grandfather sought refuge in the Catholic church, to which he converted when he married my grandmother who (though not Mexican) was both Irish and Catholic.

But who'd have thought it? A nice boy like me, 'Coming from such a wicked place north of the Border (6)'?[i]

22 APRIL 2005

i HAWICK

## *Doughnuts*

'Can areas of study define a wit? (1,1,6)'[i] Bunthorne asked last Friday. It's a good question, but I didn't really think about it until my son and I went to the grocery store yesterday.

He has become a fussy eater of late, for which I blame his teacher. It may be the National Curriculum that dictates they study nutrition this term, but only she is to blame for making it interesting.

And so from being a casual omnivore (and in this he was both a browser and a predator) he has become an obsessive reader of labels. 'Get a load of the additives in that,' he will say, before banning various food products from our household on the grounds that they 'contain too much salt' or because we 'can't be sure about the integrity of the supply chain'.

This is irritating. I am wholly in agreement with my friend Philip that one of the redeeming features of parenthood is that one can buy and eat fish fingers without feeling embarrassment or remorse. But not any more! Those halcyon days when three Pepperamis and a bag of wine gums constituted a good meal are lost for ever, consigned like the 'blue remembered hills', to the dustbin of history. Now it's all 'organic this' and 'natural that'.

This reached its nadir yesterday when a packet of chocolate digestives was rejected on the grounds that each biscuit contains four grams of fat.

'OK,' I say. 'Then what?'

He looks about the store for something that isn't condemned by its label. Fruit seems to be the only option, but then he is struck by a thought. The inkling of a smile stirs his lips.

'Can I have a doughnut?' he says. 'We don't know what's in that.'

13 MAY 2005

i W.C. FIELDS

# A Question of Faith

From time to time I light candles in churches. Usually Catholic, but not always. And I may or may not have someone in mind when I do it. It's more often a question of general loss, an act in memory of those not present. Their absence may be temporary or permanent. At London Bridge yesterday I had a few moments to spare and dropped into the quiet haven that is Southwark Cathedral. There's been a church on the site for over one thousand years. I used to go there often when my offices were around the corner, squeezed between the railway lines and Borough Market. I lit a candle for my father and then took advantage of a moment when it wasn't raining to sit in the cathedral grounds and contemplate the nature of things.

Or, which amounts to the same thing, to do the crossword. As is so often the case there was a certain serendipity to the moment. Araucaria had chosen 'Auld Lang Syne' as his theme and the solutions suited my mood. But one clue will stay with me.

My father passed away without any of the trappings of the faith in which he spent the greater part of his life. No Mass. No last rites. No repentance. None of 'that', at his request and to my considerable relief. And still I go to church to remember, and to drink, as it were, from a collective cup of kindness. And I know that my father would have paused in a moment of ambivalence on solving this clue: 'Left infirm by faith? (5)'.[i]

3 JUNE 2005

i CREDO

# A Piercing Question

You'll be pleased to know that the question of my daughter's body piercing has been amicably resolved.* We each gave a little and the position now is that she may do what she wants with her ears as and when she passes her Grade Five music examination. By my calculations this should happen some time in October, which gives her a good four months in which to change her mind. Given the rate at which her musical tastes change – the speed with which her view of McFly changed from devotion to contempt was positively unseemly – I think there is every chance that by the time she takes the exam she will regard pierced ears as a deluded affectation of the young.

And it may take longer. The exam I mean. The reason there was haggling to be done is that her musical interests have moved on from piano to guitar. This is a significant emotional shift. She can't, as it were, see a red door without wanting to paint it black. And this week I found myself forking out large amounts of cash for tickets to the next My Chemical Romance gig.

Despite this, she is not yet persuaded of the relationship between the amount of practising she does and the quality of playing she produces. While she is happy to spend hours practising various riffs on her guitar, it takes a great deal more cajoling to get her anywhere near the piano.

But we live in hope. I am sure it is only a matter of time before she decides to put in the work that will enable her to 'Shine – like Chopin? (6,6)'.[i]

And to get her ears pierced.

* See p. 79–80.

10 JUNE 2005

i FRENCH POLISH

## Sue Who?

Being as she has to travel each day to the big city to earn her daily crust, it fell this year to my girlfriend to purchase the necessary selection of puzzle anthologies to see us through the long summer evenings on the Pagasitic Gulf.

'So what do you think?' she asked, more out of politeness than interest.

I thought Araucaria would do nicely.

'Hmmm,' she said, before suggesting we might possibly have done most of the puzzles in the great man's latest collection.

'Well, all right. Get the new collection of cryptics from the *Independent*. I'm told it's very good.'

'Hmmm,' she said. 'I haven't done the *Independent* much.'

But I had, and they're excellent puzzles. But we could always try to step up a notch and get the new Chambers collection of Azed's puzzles? To date my record with Azed has been marginally worse than that of the England Cricket team playing Australia. Flashes of brilliance (well, I thought they were brilliant) followed by dismal hours in which a succession of possible solutions is sent back to the pavilion with heads bowed. Speaking of which, I see Andrew Strauss is reported to be the 'crossword champ of the dressing room'. I confidently predict that he (and we) will come good in the next Test.*

'Hmmm,' said my girlfriend. (She can really be quite irritating.) 'I was thinking maybe we'd try something new.'

Now, as I'm sure you know, when one half of a relationship suggests 'something new', there are certain to be stormy waters ahead. But what did she have in mind? Calum MacDonald's puzzles from the *Glasgow Herald*? I was up for that. The new Chambers collections of weekend puzzles from the *Independent*? Sounded good to me, even though the introduction warns us, with beautiful understatement, that readers will be 'wise to avail themselves of a good dictionary'.

But I didn't, which may be why words failed me when she returned with not one but three volumes of Sudoku.

'The kids like them,' she said, as though that was an excuse.

'Hmmm,' I replied.

* Sort of. He made forty-eight and six and took one catch (Hayden).

29 JULY 2005

# Travels With My Crossword

# Airport Signs and The Point of Things

My daughter has reached the age where she is interested to know the point of things. What, for instance, is the point of crosswords?

I found this hard to answer until I read Wednesday's 'Notes and Queries' in which Nicholas Whitehead of Newport explained that it was he who had placed a sign on the A44 in Wales directing drivers to 'Llandegley International Airport'. Of course there is no such airport, but Mr Whitehead liked the 'gentle anarchy' of the idea. He thinks of it as art and happily paid £1,000 to lease the space for a year.

Crosswords should be a haven for gentle anarchy. Adrian Bell, who set the first puzzle for *The Times* in 1931, described the process as 'more like a cinema than a reservoir. It is a sort of continuous performance of surrealist (though rigorously pertinent) imagery, related only by the interlockings and juxtapositions of orthography'.

Which brings me to Bunthorne, a man for whom life appears to be a continuous performance of surreal association. Last week he had me giggling with this preposterous (but rigorously pertinent) anagram: '"So, *qu'est à manger, Louis?*"' or, perhaps, "Is this *le chef*'s bible?" (8,13)',[i] but it was this homonym that had me transfixed by the sheer, glorious inconsequence of it all: 'More epigrammatical, say, than this oracular medium (6)'.[ii]

'Anarchy' is, of course, a slippery notion defined by some as the absence of government and by others to be the absence of any *need* for government, which is not quite the same thing. In the case of Mr Whitehead's sign, one assumes he has the former idea in mind. But in crosswords it is – or should be – the latter reading of the word that applies, and the anarchy, of course, can take many forms – in the definition, in the structure of the clue, in the juxtapositioning. Crosswords make up a utopian world, ungoverned, unstructured, chaotic and yet coherent and rewarding.

The lease for Mr Whitehead's sign is up for renewal this month. I hope he can find the £1,000 he needs to keep it there, if necessary by public subscription.

1 AUGUST 2003

i LAROUSSE GASTRONOMIQUE; ii PYTHIA

## *American crosswords*

I once came third to last in the American Crossword Tournament, which cured me of my hitherto fondly held belief that 'their' puzzles were too easy for 'us'. The key difference is that 'our' puzzles have two parts to every clue (the definition and the subsidiary route to the definition) whereas 'theirs' have only a definition. This definition may be as cryptic as you like, but since there is only one part to the clue the only way of knowing you have the right answer is to solve all the checked clues as well. Despite my position in the tournament I sometimes – just for the hell of it – argue that ours represent the high point of Western civilization whereas theirs are little more than childlike doodling.

You can see that some might find this irritating.

Which is why last week I was put in my place by a New York-based reader who used an astute combination of argument and flattery to silence me. The *New York Times*, he agreed, has fairly straightforward puzzles through the week, but on Sundays it usually has a theme and within the theme there is great scope for imagination and flair, both in the clues and in the composition of the theme and the grid.

The puzzle in question required the solver to substitute the name for a typographical or grammatical symbol for the asterisk in the clue. One particularly delightful example read 'Make Annie happy. PiY'.[i] US crosswords, irritatingly, don't give the number of letters as part of the clue, but in this case the answer needed to fill an 11-letter space. So we need a 9-letter word for a typographical symbol. Put it inside 'P' and 'Y' to get something that will make Annie happy.

Annie who? This of course is the trouble with American crosswords. We have no way of knowing which Annie … until, dimly, from some forgotten corner of our minds we dredge up the information that little orphan Annie had a dog called Sandy.

And from there it is a short step to the solution, which I urge you all to do.

29 AUGUST 2003

i PAMPER SANDY

# Tony Blair not in Ghana

I spent a couple of very enjoyable hours the other week talking about crosswords with Barbara Hall who edits and sets the puzzles for the *Sunday Times*, a job she has done for nearly thirty years. Barbara is, as far as I know, Britain's longest serving (though not quite oldest) crossword compiler. She had her first puzzle published in 1938 in what was then the *Evening News*, and has been at it pretty constantly ever since.

The stories I enjoyed most were those she told about the time she spent in Zambia, where, in addition to serving as agony aunt for the *African Mail*, she set puzzles in English and at least four other African languages. I thought of her this week when I scanned the Ghanaian papers for a crossword. I'm in Kumasi, the ancient capital of Ashanti, where I'm attending the Annual General Meeting of Kuapa Kokoo. 'Kuapa' is a cooperative of about 40,000 cocoa farmers and I helped to set up the marketing company in London that sells their brand of Fairtrade chocolate.

Well, crosswords are not that big in Ghana. On first asking I was shown *People and Places*, a kind of gossip rag that had a simple wordsearch. My hosts, unhappy at my disappointment (and clearly suspecting that the heat had diminished my tenuous grasp on reality), then rootled through all the other dailies in search of a puzzle. Nothing in the *Daily Graphic*. The cupboard of the *Daily Guide* was similarly bare. It was only when we turned, not quite in desperation, to *The Mirror* that we found Elite Word Puzzle No. 127 by Ekow Michaels.

This was a 'concise' rather than a cryptic puzzle and while some clues erred on the side of simplicity ('The capital of Kenya (7)', for instance), there were others that made me pause. 'Tony—(5).' Now that rings a bell. Tony. Tony. No, don't tell me. Tall chap. Came to Ghana once, made all sorts of promises about what he would do for African farmers and was never seen again.

Blair. That's it. Tony Blair.

26 SEPTEMBER 2003

## *Our Johns, We Johns and Their Johns*

It was a cold bright spring morning a couple of years ago and I was hopping from one foot to another on the steps of the Capitol Building in Washington DC. Earlier a friend and I had feasted unwisely on 'hopping John' (rice, peas, salt pork and any-thing else in the cupboard) with what he – but not I – thought were hilarious results.

'I need the john,' I said.

Fortunately help was at hand. Lining an entire pavement to one side of the building was a series of Portaloos thoughtfully provided by 'John's Johns'. John's john was everything I could have asked for at that moment and I emerged feeling blessed (though not necessarily by God, although this is the derivation of the name 'John').

I thought of this (you'll not be surprised to learn) while attempting last week's prize puzzle by Biggles in which the theme was buried in the second half of the solution to this clue: 'This mineral's down the toilet (4,4)'.[i]

The dictionaries of etymology that I have to hand are non-committal on how 'john' came to mean toilet. What is apparently known is that it was originally *Cousin John*. A Harvard residence rule dating from 1735 read, 'No Freshman shall go into the Fellows' Cousin John.' The dictionaries do list at least thirty-seven other uses for the word: John Doe; john, meaning a prostitute's client; various historical Johns, notably the Baptist; several popes; and a king or two of England, Hungary, Poland, Portugal and France, and so on. 'Biggles', of course, was written by W.E. Johns. What I hadn't known was that it came into the English language in various ways. In the semi-precious stone, blue john, for example, 'john' derives from 'jaune' and the stone is so-called because the layers of oil deposited in calcium fluoride give it that peculiar blue-yellow colour.

Those with longer memories will know this is not the first time *Guardian* setters have played with the word. It was only last year that Enigmatist came up with 'W.C. Fields' output? (6,6)'[ii] in a puzzle themed on precisely that.

1 OCTOBER 2003

i BLUE JOHN; ii TOILET HUMOUR

# All Shook Up

To the United States this week, where I had the curious experience of trying to explain the charms of cryptic crosswords to several nurses working in the trauma operating rooms of the

Regional Medical Center (*sic*) at Memphis, better known as 'The Med'. I have tried this before and it is not easy, especially if your audience does not already do crosswords.

But I am nothing if not willing in the service of my cause. And besides we had a little down time to kill on the night shift while waiting for another trauma victim (defined as someone who is 'bent, broke or bleeding') to come through the doors.

There was a problem. The only puzzle I had brought with me was Cyclops' latest offering in *Private Eye*. No matter, I thought. Let's give it a go.

The trouble with Cyclops is you have to get past the smut and so the first reasonably clean clue (i.e. not containing words such as 'tosser', 'sex', 'piss-up' and so on) was, 'US government's bloody useless small-minded hostile initiatives and bureaucratic activity (4,14)'.[i]

Since Tennessee has a Democrat governor and Memphis is a safely Democrat city, I was confident that this clue would appeal to my audience and I launched smoothly into my spiel. 'What you do is you look for the definition…'

'They got that right,' said a laconic male nurse when we solved it. Like many safety-net hospitals in the US, the Med faces constant funding pressure and threats of closure. 'What else you got?'

Our attention was drawn – perhaps inevitably – to another clue that seemed to say something about America: 'Hired help with heater protects many an American (7)'.[ii]

We worked that one out too, but the same male nurse objected to the definition. 'You wouldn't say that if you saw what I saw,' he said. What he saw – and what I have seen for much of this year while researching a book at the Med – is the steady stream of 'bent, broke and bleeding' gunshot victims who are brought to the hospital.

And handguns have never protected them.

31 OCTOOBER 2003

i BUSH ADMINISTRATION; ii HANDGUN

---

# The World in a Grain of Sand

'To see a World in a Grain of Sand/And Heaven in a Wild Flower/Hold Infinity in the palm of your hand/And Eternity in an hour.' Blake's formulation of the poetic impulse has long seemed to me to describe the crossword setter's task as well. What makes them good – along with rigorous attention to detail, fairness and so on – is their ability to take not an oxymoron exactly, but something that we might describe as a 'radical juxtapositioning' of competing ideas and turn them into a clue greater than the sum of its disparate parts.

Mind you, an hour spent looking at a Bunthorne puzzle without getting a single solution may well feel like an eternity. And one can't help looking at phrases like 'Wild Flower' with a degree of suspicion. What is this? An anagram indicator? A river? In fact, the whole stanza looks like a series of crossword clues. The lines have that disquieting rhythm to them that has you looking for a definition before you remember it's only a poem.

But I digress. Yesterday Bunthorne took us on a tour of the world, starting – in my case at least – with a word that entered the language only when South Africa left the Commonwealth in 1961 and the rand – or 'No order for unordered currency (4)' if you prefer – became the monetary unit of the new Republic of South Africa. My friend who works at the Finance Ministry in Pretoria and who does the *Guardian* puzzles online wanted reassurance that 'unordered' was not a slur on the rand's desirability in the world's currency markets.

Bunthorne's puzzle had as solutions several words only recently included in English dictionaries. It was shortly after the rand became common currency that we in the West started taking an interest in Japanese massage. As far as I know the two are not related. Except, of course, in a Bunthorne puzzle when clues like 'About time some Muslim backed American pressure on Japanese (7)'[i] enable us to see the world in what is no more than a grain of sand.

12 DECEMBER 2003

i SHIATSU

---

## *Edinburgh Calling*

To Edinburgh last weekend where I was researching what pass for my roots and where my uncle managed to retrieve from the attic the birth, death and marriage certificates of a fine range of previously unheralded relatives, including my late great-uncle Wully. He played for Jed Forest rugby club in the years after the Boer War and was briefly considered a prospect for Scotland.

The conversation moved on, as it might, to my uncle's cousin who farms near Eskdalemuir. She is getting on a bit now and is, my uncle told me in an unexpected but wholly welcome example of Scottish rhyming slang, 'a bit corned beef'.

It took me a while to work out that north of the border 'beef' rhymes with 'deaf'.

'And anyway,' said my aunt, 'actually he means "blind".'

Saying one thing while meaning quite another is, of course, the essence of crossword clues in which, in Afrit's famous injunction, the setter: 'may attempt to mislead by employing a form of words which can be taken in more than one way, and it is the solver's fault if he takes it the wrong way but it is the setter's fault if he cannot logically take it the right way.'

I thought of this as I grappled with one down in yesterday's puzzle by Brummie: 'Heads unwelcome visitors after school: without enthusiasm, one leaves cutlets (10)',[i] in which everything except the definition conspired to point the unwary solver in the wrong direction. Elsewhere it was the definition that was designed to mislead. 'City venue occasionally spotlighting tattoo artists (9,6)'[ii] is a little daunting unless you have recently been in Edinburgh. In the same puzzle I quite liked '"Subtly shaded nude composition" admits party (7)'.[iii] You had to cast your net a little wider than usual to get party = ANC.

Alternatively you get modest in-jokes like the clue in Mudd's puzzle in the *Financial Times* last Saturday: 'Snipe's excited body part (5)'.[iv]

There are two possible answers, but it is entirely your fault if you opt for the smutty one.

20 FEBRUARY 2004

i SCHNITZELS; ii EDINBURGH CASTLE; iii NUANCED; iv SPINE

# *How to Gut a Son*

More squeamish readers may want to look away now.

As male bonding rituals go, the old 'how-to-gut-a-fish' routine ranks far higher in my estimation that the 'little chats' fathers are sometimes required to have with their sons. Even so, when my son plucked his first fish from the freezing waters of Kamchatka last week, I was only too happy to let his uncle do the talking, while I lay back in the hot waters of the thermal springs and cursed myself for not having brought any crosswords.

But we were (as Araucaria put it yesterday) 'Well protected with forelimbs on child (male) and choppers (5,2,3,5)' [i] and what follows is verbatim:

'You take the knife ...'

'The big one?'

'... when you catch a big fish. For the moment the small one is fine. And you stick it in that hole there. No, not that hole. The other one.'

'This one?'

'Yes.'

'Yuck! What's that?'

'Well, that hole is its bum and that stuff is ...'

'Really?' (My son peers more closely to see that it really is ...)

'Now cut all the way up the stomach. Make sure you have the blade pointing away from yourself. Away!'

'Ow.'

Silence. But my son soon loses interest in his pain and focuses on the stuff falling out of the fish.

'What's that?'

'That's its guts.'

At this point my Russian friend arrives. Confronted by the unlikely sight of two near-naked foreigners messing about with – or rather, in – fish gore, she does the sensible thing and takes away the knife. 'You should clean his cut,' she says severely, which was correct but entirely beside the point. Unless she was talking about the fish.

'Rats,' said my son, who agrees with Janus that 'Sometimes it is no advantage to include a girl (3,3,5)'.[ii]

17 SEPTEMBER 2004

i ARMED TO THE TEETH; ii NOW AND AGAIN

## Bolshoi Ballet

Muscovites love their crosswords. You see them at it everywhere, even in the grand atrium of the Bolshoi Theatre, where I was amused on Sunday to see a man in a curious lilac suit chewing his pencil as he stewed on a clue. We were there for a performance of Shostakovich's little known work, *The Bright Stream*. The ballet was first staged in 1935 but quickly fell foul of the Soviet authorities, who took offence at the light-hearted libretto. 'A serious theme requires serious treatment and hard and conscientious work,' a *Pravda* editorial intoned before going on to dismiss the ballet as 'slapdash, lacking character and expressing nothing.' Since the main action of *The Bright Stream* concerns a series of romantic misunderstandings between workers on a collective farm and artistes from the city whose libidos have momentarily got the better of their socialist sensibilities, this is perhaps not surprising. The final scene in which workers and artistes realize they share a common interest in building socialism (I'm quoting…) was not enough to save the ballet. It had been performed only eleven times before the *Pravda* editorial consigned it to the dustbin of history.

Which is where we now seem to live, for the current revival is playing to delighted full houses. It profits from extraordinary performances, especially that of Nikolay Tsiskaridze who has to dance almost the entire second act dressed as a woman in a costume that might well have inspired this clue from Wednesday's *Times*: 'Eye-catching and shockingly indiscreet (10)'.[i] And I loved the gleefully ironic interpretation given by choreographer Alexei Ratmansky to this homage to the Soviet dream. Shostakovich, of course, knew the dangers. His previous attempts at 'Soviet Ballet' had similarly failed to please the authorities and it may be that another bad review unwittingly identified why. The composer was held to have 'written music to his own, private thoughts which are more significant and profound than is the libretto'.

And we all know how dangerous private thoughts are, especially profound ones. Which made me wonder at the smile playing on the lips of the man in the lilac suit.

26 NOVEMBER 2004

i IRIDESCENT

# Passport Stamps

Do you know where you were on 22 December 2003? Or 7 November 1990? And how? Some people keep diaries, others keep letters…and some make notes in the margins of their crossword collections. It was many years ago – 1968 in fact – when David Cutler moved to Washington DC to take up a post with the International Monetary Fund. As with many British people in the United States he found his accent to be a considerable advantage, and in his retirement he now finds work reading books onto tape for visually impaired people to enjoy.

And, like many exiles, whether voluntary or not, he finds he misses 'our' crosswords. He learned how to do them from his father who was, so he tells me, 'a *Telegraph* man who, when he reached the end of his tether would turn to me and say "Go on, give us a push." And usually I could, but I hated him explaining the clues to me. I wanted to approach them with a fresh mind.'

In any case the training seems to have worked because David can still recall clearly the first (and only – which puts him one ahead of me) time he completed a Ximenes puzzle.

David likes to do puzzles when he is on the move and now he has found a solution: he takes a collection of *Sunday Times* puzzles with him wherever he goes and is in the habit of jotting down in the margin where and when he was solving it. 'Hilton Hotel, Nairobi, 4 December 1990,' reads one such entry. 'Heathrow / Dulles, 22 December 2003,' reads another. 'Some quite good clues in that one,' he notes. 'Not bad at all.' And by way of example he quotes this clue: 'Moves near an impartial legislator (15)'.[i] Impartial? Surely not, I hear you cry. But it is the crossword collection as document of record that appeals to me. The book has become, in effect, a diary of his travels, as reliable as – and more legible than – the stamps in his passport.

10 DECEMBER 2004

i PARLIAMENTARIAN

---

## *A Perfect Thought*

It is the kind of bright clean morning that you get only after the storm has passed. The Tuscan mountainside on which we find ourselves is alive with the whispers of a thousand impromptu streams as the rainwater from the previous night begins its long journey to the sea. Above us the azure sky lightens as the sun climbs while all around the olive groves steam faintly in the unexpected winter warmth.

My friend Dominick and I have wandered further into the valley than we intended. He is a philosopher by trade and a campaigner on disarmament by profession, or perhaps it is the other way round. In any case, there is a pattern to the walks we take over these rolling hills of southern Tuscany. Having had the whole night to read and think he arrives at my door brimming with ideas that he cannot wait to share. Out of habit he inquires, much as a parent might ask a child whether he has cleaned his teeth, whether I have read some learned work or other. He is expecting the answer 'no', but if I say 'yes', he will want me to open my mouth so that he can check. On balance both he and I prefer the answer to be 'no'.

From time to time I hold my own by quoting crossword clues. I find it gives the illusion of intelligent life.

He has been reading Dante in the Dorothy Sayers translation and as we walk he talks about Dante's view that you get what you deserve. For Dante, man is a responsible being. Whether you land in Hell or in Purgatory, you get what you choose. If you insist on having your own way, rather than God's, you will get it. In Hell. For ever. When every allowance is made (and Dante makes generous allowances) the consequences of sin are the sinner's.

'Ah,' I say knowledgeably. 'A "perfect but inconclusive thought (4)".'[i]

For I am tickled pink to find that this clue, from Monday's *FT*, was composed by a setter calling himself Dante.

31 DECEMBER 2004

i IDEA

---

# *Revolving Revolutionaries*

'When men are able to influence so many others through their life and their example, they do not die,' Aleida Guevara March wrote of her father, the doctor, finance minister and hero of the revolution, Ernesto Guevara. It also helps to have a nickname that crossword setters find useful.

I have been reading Guevara's *The African Dream: The Diaries of the Revolutionary War in the Congo*, which Tariq Ali, with some justification, called 'the balance sheet of a disaster' and which leaves one with a deep sense of the comic ineptitude of both the movement lead by the future president, Laurent Kabila and of Cuban attempts to help it. Guevara, towards the end of the diaries, tries to assess what went wrong. His conclusion, clearly heartfelt, is twofold. The first is that the peasants of the eastern Congo in the 1960s were not ready to be helped; since land was already divided amongst them, there was no need for land reform and since they appeared unwilling to take part in a cash, let alone credit, economy (Guevara bemoans the fact that the peasants ate everything they grew instead of selling it), there was little the would-be revolutionaries could do there.

And yet there was a 'war of liberation' in progress, with armies of different types going hither and thither and, from time to time, shooting at each other, and it is in this context that Guevara concludes that really it was better for the Cubans to go home and have a spanking good think. 'I think some deep thought and research needs to be devoted to the problem of revolutionary tactics where the relations of production do not give rise to land hunger among the peasantry,' he writes. Finally he turns his critical eye on himself. 'I set off with more faith than ever in the guerrilla struggle, yet we failed. My responsibility is great.'

For all the catalogue of errors, misunderstandings and incompetence, he leaves the Congo at the end of 1965 with what Araucaria only yesterday called 'A revolutionary's yearning (4)'[i] undiminished.

28 JANUARY 2005

i ACHE

# The Naked Ape

To Westlea Primary School in Seaham, County Durham last Friday for a wonderful few hours working on a project to create a crossword map of the north-east of England. The idea is that children from a local school will investigate names, places and words associated with the three major rivers of the area. And then make clues for them. The clues will fit into a grid mapping the course of the Tyne, Tees and Wear rivers. Alec Finlay, Beth Rowson and Ira Lightman had the idea, got support from Creative Partnerships and invited me along to help.

It was a delight. I had one hour flat to explain the basics of four different kinds of clues – charades, anagrams, embedded clues and 'beginnings', in which the solution consists of the first letters of a number of other words.

The kids loved it. They got the point of crosswords immediately, and soon we were making clues for everything and anything. Yarm, for example, is a small town on the north bank of the Tees. At least that's what the atlas says. What the year four and five kids of Seaham know is that Yarm is an anagram of army, Mary and Myra, is embedded in my arm, and has the beginnings of your Aunt Rita's monkey.

Quite why Aunt Rita had a monkey was left unexplored.

And then I started to show off. Give me a word, I cried. Any word! And I will make a clue! Instantly! 'Hippopotamus,' shouted the bright spark at the front. Quick as a very slow flash I came up with, 'Hi, Pop. Must stop! Crazy animal! (12)'. The kids were very impressed until the bright spark – and Ira – pointed out I had one letter too many – and another letter wrong.

And so the emperor stood naked again.

24 JUNE 2005

# SETTERS AND SOLVERS

# Losing Gracefully

To Lord's last week where I spent a very enjoyable few hours watching Andrew Flintoff smack Pollock and Ntini to all parts of the globe and discussing crosswords with an eminent setter and his girlfriend.

'You were right,' she said. 'Men are hopeless at calling out clues. He tries his on me all the time and he never says the number of letters.'

The setter had the decency to look sheepish.

'And the worst thing is,' she continued, 'when I say "How many letters?" he says, "That would make it too easy."'

'Well, it would,' said the setter, which did not necessarily advance his case.

'Yeah, right,' she replied, demonstrating conclusively that two positives can make a negative.

But the setter – or at least his mind – had already left us for that lonely place crossword setters go, and I don't think he heard. Because moments later he reappeared in the real world with this: 'Batsman says "get lost" with stuffing'.[i]

'How many letters!?' we asked in unison.

There were eight and we soon agreed that while the clue had a certain urban charm it would not be appropriate for any of the sober broadsheets (or even the *Guardian*) for which the setter works. It reminded me of a previous clue by the same setter:

'With which to admit in France that's just not cricket (8)'.[ii]

This was the setter's girlfriend's first visit to Lord's and I am sure I can say without giving offence that her grasp of the rules was, ah, sketchy.

'Well, it's not surprising,' she said. 'I learned everything I know about cricket from crosswords. They're so similar. You never know who is winning – until the end.'

Well, yes. Except when South Africa have a first innings score of 509.

8 AUGUST 2003

i FLINTOFF; ii PASSPORT

## Show me the Money

To Scotland last week where my son and I explored something of our roots by retracing the journey taken by David Balfour in Robert Louis Stevenson's *Kidnapped*. It took us from Iona (though strictly speaking it should have been Earraid) across Mull and Rannoch Moor before we headed south to Balquhidder and the Queensferry. But, unlike David who fetches up in Edinburgh to claim his inheritance, I found myself at the International Book Festival to face an hour of questions from crossword fans.

The event was a sell-out, which even I know owes more to the enduring appeal of crosswords than to my own modest charms.

The most heartfelt question came from Nick Clarke, who normally does duty as an intelligent and incisive presenter of *The World at One*. But he now revealed that he shares the insecurity of most crossword solvers. Could I, he wondered, offer any hope to people like him who have been submitting prize crosswords for twenty years without ever having won a dictionary? Or even a ballpoint pen?

Nope. I couldn't.

But I could tell him he is not alone in his misery. He probably knew that from the murmur of consensus that rippled around the room.

In a discussion afterwards though, a group agreed that the only prize worth competing for was that in *Private Eye*, which doesn't waste time with dictionaries and pens (let's face it: most crossword solvers have several of each already) but offers £100 cash for anyone who can work their way into Cyclops' tortured mind. And given that *Private Eye*'s circulation is smaller than most broadsheets, your chances of winning must be that much better.

It did make me have a look at the names of the five people (actually six; one entry came from two people) who won the prize in the *Guardian* this week. I had struggled with Bunthorne that week and I wondered whether anyone would have finished it at all. But there they were in black-and-white.

It's enough to make one 'Give up grub? Cyclops can! (5,2,2)',[i] as Cyclops once said.

15 AUGUST 2003

i CHUCK IT IN

# The Benches of Hampstead Heath (1)

There is something infinitely poignant about a person doing the prize crossword after the solution has been published. But there she was last Tuesday, sitting on a bench on Hampstead Heath and wrestling with Araucaria's bank holiday special. It's one of my favourite places too. While the kids cycle around the pond, I can do a puzzle.

We started chatting. 'Don't you ever give up?' I asked, but it was not crosswords that concerned her.

'They wouldn't let me have arms,' she said. 'And they wouldn't let me put it where she liked to sit.' I nodded sympathetically. There have been times in my life when I felt that I was unreasonably restrained from having arms.

Though these were not the sort of arms the woman in turquoise had in mind. She was talking about a bench, and the people who would not let her have arms were the Corporation of London, which nowadays allows only a certain type of bench on the Heath, the sort without arms.

Which her mother hated.

'She died last month.'

'I'm so sorry.'

She turned back to her puzzle and I found myself hoping she would never finish it. 'I suppose it's a bit like the inscriptions on benches,' she mused. 'There is a whole lot that is common knowledge about them, but the deepest associations are completely private.

'Take this puzzle. It's got some hidden message going around the edge. I'm sure it means something to Araucaria, but will it to me? Who knows?'

Well, I knew. The 'message' was 'The hand that rocked the cradle has kicked the bucket.' In the puzzle it was linked to another saying: 'One is one and all alone and evermore shall be so.'

Indeed.

But I couldn't tell her that, just as I couldn't begin to grasp the layers and layers of meaning it would have for her when she got it.

And that's the thing about crosswords. They are partly very private, partly very public, a bit like the games my children were playing on their bicycles on the other side of the pond.

5 SEPTEMBER 2003

## On Having Beautiful Buttocks

You hear them say it on television quizzes from time to time. Even Jeremy Paxman – who should know better – is prone to asking the question on *University Challenge*: 'How do you know that?' Invariably the answer is 'I just do', but equally invariably the person asked scrabbles around in their memory bank and comes up with some implausible reason why they should know a particularly obscure piece of information.

'My Aunty Doris used to keep some in the cellar,' for example. Or, 'I wrote a book on it once.'

I like to think I am above such inanities and I was dismayed therefore to find myself asking the same question last Monday. We were at the Oval at the time, watching the England cricket team cruise to a famous and thoroughly enjoyable victory over South Africa. I am not normally in the habit of bunking off work, but since this victory was about as unlikely as a giant asteroid hitting Milton Keynes, normal rules did not apply. And besides, a crossword setter (whose 'eminence', I discover, is a matter of some debate) had invited me.

So it was that during the lunch break we had a go at the Audreus puzzle in that morning's *Guardian*. There were five of us in the group and since this was a social occasion we took it in turns, with each person completing one clue and then passing the puzzle on to the next. A pattern soon emerged: everyone was doing the relatively easy stuff around the edges and avoiding the long anagram that formed the spine of the puzzle: 'You'll cap GIs anyhow by having beautiful buttocks (11)'.

Well, almost everyone. The setter's girlfriend had a secretive smile as she watched us each in turn struggle with what was obviously an anagram – but without an obvious answer.

Eventually, when the rest of us had given up, she filled in the solution. It was 'callipygous'.

'But how do you know that it means 'having beautiful buttocks'?' I asked.

'Because I do,' she replied sweetly.

'She does,' said the setter knowledgeably.

12 SEPTEMBER 2003

# A New Setter

One of the characteristics of crossword compilers is their longevity and it is not often therefore that a new one swims into our ken. Not since Paul's debut in 1995 have we had a new *Guardian* pseudonym to contend with. And the editor recently declared that he is keen to keep numbers down, lest we (being simple solvers) lose track of who is whom. But now we have two newcomers: first there was Brummie who had his second puzzle published a couple of weeks back, and then – making a debut splash with the prize puzzle – Imogen appeared last Saturday.

In a series of rather entertaining clues around the edge of the puzzle, Brummie seemed to be expressing his nervousness at what he must know – he has had puzzles published elsewhere – is the setter's lot. One across was a 'Closing time of special significance (3,3,2,2,3)'[i] and the other answers around the edges of the puzzle were 'egg on one's face', 'baptism of fire' and 'as sick as a parrot'.

Imogen preferred to open with a homophone, which I regard as a highly risky business for a setter. Brian Greer, who used to edit the puzzles for *The Times* once complained that English setters – he is Irish – pronounced 'for', four' and 'fore' in the same way whereas any self-respecting Irish person knows they have three distinct pronunciations. One might – if like me you have an accent other than RP – make a similar complaint about 'Slow runner, say, the French salute (8)'.[ii]

Mind you, I dimly recollect that Paul used the same technique for the same solution a year or so ago. 'Standard for leaking hosepipe to be reported (9)' is a testing clue for anyone who speaks with any accent other than a southern graduate drawl.

So it was not with a wild surmise that I tried the puzzle on Saturday, but nor was I disappointed. The theme was neatly constructed and pleasantly devious, and it took me a while to get it except that I, too, have a 'Writer's fondness for fine fabric (8)'.[iii]

24 October 2003

i THE END OF AN ERA; ii TRICOLOUR; iii LOVELACE

---

## *French Texts*

'Help!' said the text message. '19 dn. Bastard.'

In this context 'bastard' was a reference to the setter rather than to me or to my friend stranded in the south of France with only a husband-who-doesn't-do-crosswords, a wild west wind and Araucaria's Christmas prize puzzle for company.

Three minutes later another message came. 'Also 23 ac, 13 ac, 42 ac and 23 dn. Bugger.'

We spoke on the phone. 'Bastard,' she said, not for the first time. I could hear her husband saying something from what sounded like a crowded bar. 'He says he'll pay cash,' she said, 'if you help me finish it.'

You can imagine the scene. Huddled in a corner table of a small bistro overlooking the old port in Monte Carlo, her husband is not in the best of moods. For a start he's suffering from a persistent flu that, despite the application of several glasses of medicinal whisky, refuses to go away. Then there's the fact that his '*pièce de boeuf*' ('Literally,' says my friend with a sniff; she's not a fan of the new gastronomy) costs almost as much as he lost at the casino the night before. And then there's this bloody puzzle.

He blows his nose mournfully.

Well I like to be helpful, even in a puzzle in which we are warned that most solutions 'contain an animal which is ignored in the subsidiary part of the clue'. And beside, someone is offering to pay cash to ransom his wife from her servitude to Araucaria's whimsy.

But some time (it may have been hours; it may have been days) later I am no nearer the answer. And nor are my friends. On the other hand his flu seems to be getting worse and another cold front is sweeping in from the west. From the bag of medicines he's carrying he takes a particularly potent-looking combination and knocks it back. He begins to feel drowsy.

'Swallowed a tablet? Ring the bell (4,1,4),'[i] says my friend, which I suddenly realize must be the most imaginative use ever of 'okapi' in a crossword puzzle.

2 JANUARY 2004

i TOOK A PILL

## *Advocaat*

My late father was a practical man. 'Right,' he would say of a long winter's evening. 'Who wants to do this jigsaw with me? Clear the table, get a hammer and we're ready to start.'

On Monday I found a discarded copy of Monday's *Daily Telegraph*, in which there was evidence of a solver who had attempted to do the puzzle with the aid of a hammer. You could read the story from his desperate doodles around the puzzle.

It all started well enough. No need for a hammer for the top left- and right-hand sectors. It was in the bottom right-hand corner that it all started to unravel. First up was what should have been a relatively simply double definition: 'Dutch barrister's liqueur (8).' ADVOCATE wrote our solver. One can almost see him – or her, but to my mind this was a man – speeding up. He's nearing the end and he might just get it done before he arrives at Moorgate.

So ADVOCATE gives him four 'checked letters'. The first 'A' works fine, as does the 'V'. And the 'C' of 'I respect new evidence of settlements (8)'[i] similarly provides no problems. The last checked letter from ADVOCATE is the 'T' which he now sees fits into the pattern _ E _ T P _ _ R _ . And the clue? The clue is 'These, when mixed, harm poets (9)'.

Well, it doesn't look hard, he thinks. Clearly an anagram of 'harm poets'. Easy. Metaphors. But the trouble is that 'metaphors' doesn't fit. We see his other attempts around the edge of the puzzle. He writes the letters of 'harm poets' no less than five times. Sometimes in a 3 x 3 grid. Twice in a circle. He tries words that die before he's finished. 'EARSHO…' and 'SHORTE…' And finally he reaches for the hammer. MEATPHORS, he writes. But he is disgusted with himself and he doesn't fill in the only other missing answer: 'It's just a question of time (4)'.[ii]

I sympathize with this anonymous solver. Who amongst us has not been there? It's enough to make one drink ADVO-CAAT.

23 JANUARY 2004
i RECEIPTS; ii WHEN

## *Mirror, Mirror on the Wall*

I am on record as thinking that Araucaria is the best thing since baked beans, but even I could not suppress a twinge of sympathy for Mike Gribbin. He wrote to the *Guardian* last week to celebrate the fact that he had – for the first time ever – completed crossword puzzles on successive days. The setters in question were Rufus and Rover. Hoping for a third he opened the paper on the Wednesday only to find the puzzle was by 'bloody Araucaria and that was the end of that'.

Of course, Araucaria has his defenders and a letter rounding up the usual adjectives (challenging, witty, glorious, etc.) duly appeared last Tuesday.

Now crossword setting is a dismal and difficult art and it will always be the case that one solver's delight is another's despair. It is exactly one year since I made my one and only foray into this dangerous field. The occasion was last year's London Book Fair and I set a puzzle for *Publishing News*. The idea was that all those agents and publishers would use their free time to do the puzzle, and the first correct entry would win a bottle of champagne.

The sad truth is that no one finished it. I like to think this is because they were too busy, but I suspect that I made the cardinal setting error: in my effort to be witty I was opaque and in my desire to be clever I was impenetrable.

This year *Publishing News* had no need of my art for Jordan had deigned to put in an appearance at the Fair, and, as they put it, she 'didn't take anything off at photocall for her forthcoming John Blake book, but a lot of photographers nearly fell off the Gallery in their eagerness to snap as much of the model as they could.'

And so it was left to Paul on Wednesday to pose the conundrum facing all solvers: 'Newspapers like pin-ups – Araucaria, Rufus…which is the most sporting? It's a question of vanity (6,6,2,3,4,3,2,3,7,2,4,3).'[i]

Well, I know what I think – and it isn't Jordan.

19 MARCH 2004

i MIRROR, MIRROR ON THE WALL,
WHO IS THE FAIREST OF THEM ALL?

## *Your Monet or your Life*

We were in the National Gallery in Trafalgar Square and my son closed his eyes. It was not the sight of several scantily-clad nudes of Rubenesque proportions that put him off. Rather it was a lecture I had given him recently on how to render images more memorable. An 'Opportunity for son to make out (5)',[i] as Chifonie put it in yesterday's puzzle.

'Look at it,' I instructed him. 'Then close your eyes. Then open, close, open, close. And the image will be stuck in your mind.'

'I tried it,' he said. 'Definitely it was a foul. The ref. was cheating.' This is a tense time, you understand, for Arsenal fans.

But standing in the gallery I recalled a discussion of setting styles I had recently with a setter.

'Sometimes colours come to mind,' he said. 'I don't know why. Bunthorne, for example. He always seems purple to me. I think of Bunthorne as someone like Francis Bacon and I suppose Rufus is Monet.'

Well, how very flattering.

'The thing is, I'd rather look at a picture of someone being slaughtered than a bunch of out-of-focus water lilies any time.'

I'm not sure I would, but it poses a good question. Why do we do crossword puzzles? Are we, like my friend the setter, more interested in violence, or are we seeking solace in a pastoral idyll, whether or not it is in focus?

My advice is not to trust the person who thinks there is an easy answer to this question.

As we left the gallery my son gave the paintings one more glance.

'Well, that was interesting,' I said.

'If you say so,' he demurred.

'Which one will you remember most?' I asked as we passed Seurat's Parisienne bathers. Across the room van Gogh's sunflowers wilted under my son's withering gaze.

'There was one I liked,' he said. 'The one where the man got his head chopped off.'

'Oh.'

'But it's good you brought me,' he added. 'Now I won't have to waste time coming when I'm older.'

As Chifonie said, a 'Rare appreciation of parent (4)'.[ii]

26 MARCH 2004
i SCOPE; ii REAR

## *Pseuds and Pseudonyms*

The column in which I reported how someone always thought of Bunthorne as 'purple', elicited an unusually high number of letters and e-mails from readers, several of which went on to describe the images various solvers have of the *Guardian*'s stable of setters. Perhaps the most poignant came from one solver – she is eighty-nine years old and has been doing crosswords since 'before the '39 war' – who writes that she has a vivid picture derived from the pseudonyms of each solver. 'Probably if I asked around I could get an actual likeness, but I'd rather see them as I've drawn them. That way I am at liberty to direct masses of abuse at their heads especially when I'm quite unable to ascertain what the S.O.B.s are driving at ...'

Well, indeed. And who amongst us doesn't?

But it does make you wonder a little at the stories behind the pseudonyms. Some, like Araucaria (the monkey puzzle tree), Bunthorne (the operetta character) and Enigmatist seem fairly self-explanatory. Brummie comes from Birmingham and Gemini makes sense when you know that it is not one but two people. But Shed?

It wasn't always this way. The late John Perkin introduced pseudonyms for *Guardian* setters and once told me that they were to be both 'a promise and a warning to solvers'. His example was followed by publications like the *FT* and the *Independent*, but *The Times* and the *Telegraph* maintain their tradition of anonymity. It's a difference of emphasis. Having pseudonyms allows the *Guardian* to celebrate the diversity of its setters. By contrast the point at *The Times*, their crossword editor once told me (pointedly), 'was to create a *Times* crossword, not a puzzle by someone special that *The Times* happens to carry.'

I have not met Crispa, but I know that she is both almost as old as my correspondent and one of the few women to set for the *Guardian*. She has been setting for several decades and clearly has no truck with impatient solvers.

'Their patrons must expect to get needled (10)'[i] she said on Monday.

9 APRIL 2004
i TATTOOISTS

## Overtrumps

Owing to a slight misunderstanding that is (I confess) entirely to do with my inability to pay attention and stick to the conventions, my partner and I have ended up in a contract of six diamonds with only seven trumps between us. It seems hopeless, but we are playing duplicate bridge and so one can't simply throw in the hand. At least we aren't doubled. So I ruff the spade lead in dummy and set about trying to lose only one trick in trumps before running the clubs in which suit we enjoy an 11–2 majority.

I mention this only because my partner sets puzzles in the *Guardian*, the *Financial Times* and *The Times* and earlier (when we were still talking…) he mentioned how often bridge metaphors and phrases find their way into crossword puzzles. It's almost as bad as cricket.

'Last week, for example,' he says, referring to last Friday's Araucaria, 'there was this clue: "Clear behind? Go still higher at bridge (9)".[i] Of course,' he goes on, 'I've done the same thing myself.' And although he is not one of those setters who like to quote their clues at every opportunity, he mentions one he set recently: 'Hardly the bottom bid in bridge (2,5).'[ii]

But not all bridge clues rely on using 'rump' to mean 'backside'.

Back to the game. Miraculously the diamonds have split 3–3. All I need now is a spade lead to my ace and I can play out the clubs. Instead, the dreaded heart lead comes but – also miraculously (or 'like a bloody idiot' according to his partner) – my opponent ducks and I win with the queen. The clubs should be easy. Unblock the ace, finesse the queen and run like the wind.

Which I do.

Earlier in the week I was playing with Araucaria. We have not yet managed to bid *and* make what Rufus called 'the achievement of one who does not miss a trick (5,4)',[iii] but I am sure it is only a matter of time for one who has spent 'a lifetime in bridge (4)'.[iv]

23 APRIL 2004

i OVERTRUMP; ii NO TRUMP; iii GRAND SLAM; iv SPAN

# The Benches of Hampstead Heath (2)

Deep in the heart of South Africa's sugar estates lies the small town of Eshowe, in the middle of which is the Dlinza Forest, famous for the opportunity it offers birdwatchers to see the spotted ground thrush and other rare birds. There is an elevated walkway that reaches out from the steep incline of a hill and enables the visitor to walk above the treetops. And at each stage it is possible to see the vegetation indigenous to this part of the world, plants like umzimbeet, ironplum and wild strangler figs.

The forest is so named because it is on the site of an ancient burial ground of the Sibiya dynasty, and in isiZulu 'dlinza' means sepulchre or grave. But in one of those verbal felicities at which isiZulu excels, the verb from which the noun derives means something more complicated. It describes a multi-layered response to death, including acts of remembrance, but also meditation and thought.

Walking on Hampstead Heath early yesterday I took note of the inscriptions on the benches, which people have dedicated to the memory of people who have died. I'm told that there are some 700 such benches on the Heath, of which there are two that appeal to me particularly. These are the two that, in contravention of the form, had been dedicated prior to the death of the person concerned. 'Albert Thomas Green,' read one inscription, 'still alive and kicking.' 'Gentle neighbour sigh not yet,' said the other, inscribed only to 'Ben W. 1912–, I've only gone to Somerset.'

I sat on Ben's bench to tackle what remained of Araucaria's Wednesday puzzle, at the heart of which was one of those extended anagrams that crop up from time to time. Except it was more than that... '4 – hot gelignite and hot TNT go unstable leading to double 13 (2,3,2,6,4,4,4,5)' where 4 was 'STAY PUT' and 13 was 'RAGE'.[i]

Pre-dedicating your bench struck me as one way to rage against the dying of the light, even though in Albert Green's case someone had added the inevitable ending:

'But now sadly missed (14.10.96).'

14 MAY 2004

i DO NOT GO GENTLE INTO THAT GOOD NIGHT

## *Noo Mangat*

It was a name to conjure with. Amongst the Phillips, Stewards and Jacksons, M. Noo Mangat of Newark, USA raised his head above the parapet and claimed one of the five dictionaries on offer for solving *Guardian* Prize Puzzle number 23,161. A name to conjure with – and an address too. What was someone in Newark, Delaware doing winning prizes for a British cryptic crossword puzzle?

I remembered the puzzle. It had a series of clues in which the definition was a number from one to twelve, which turned out to be signs of the zodiac. I remembered it also because I almost completed it. I was only two clues short: 'A little room to escape in unsociable style (7)'[i] is hardly a stretch, but I blanked it completely and so did not have the checked 'F' which would have helped me to solve 'Sent for something that's irrecoverable (7,3)',[ii] a clue I was sure I would like if only I could do it.

Noo Mangat wasn't at home, but his wife assured me he would be delighted to hear from me. 'He's crazy about those puzzles,' she said. 'He says they're so much better than ours.' I got through to him at the office and we quickly ran through the generations. His grandparents came to Britain from India in the 1930s. His parents followed shortly after the war and he was born here not long after that. As a youth – 'we took the *Mirror* then' – he taught himself to do simple crosswords. When his parents moved to the *Guardian*, he did too and a long apprenticeship followed. He had no teacher and instead worked backwards from the solutions. When, as a student, he left for the US, it was with strict instructions that his parents should clip the puzzles and send them to him in batches. He talked like a man who had lost something, but wasn't sure what.

'I never leave home without one,' he told me, even though he had, in one sense, left home a long time ago. It's not irrecoverable, I thought, if you can take it with you.

18 JUNE 2004

i ALOOFLY; ii WRITTEN OFF

## *Omar Khayyám, honest*

By all accounts – although the accounts I have in mind are those of the *Cambridge Guide to Literature in English* and the moving story in W.G. Sebald's unforgettable meditation on loss and decline, *The Rings of Saturn* – Edward FitzGerald, translator of

*The Rubáiyát of Omar Khayyám*, was a strange and lonely man.

The *Guide* tells us that FitzGerald pursued no career after leaving Cambridge and that the 'even tenor' of his life, which he spent in a small cottage in the family estate in Suffolk, was disturbed only by an incautious marriage to the daughter of a Quaker poet. The marriage lasted less than a year and Sebald speculates, with some justification it would seem, that at least part of the reason must have been the deep love that FitzGerald harboured for his friend and correspondent William Browne. For FitzGerald, Browne was the personification of an ideal and 'for that very reason he seemed overshadowed by mortality from the start,' a feeling only confirmed when Browne subsequently married and when in 1859 he died a painful death in a hunting accident. It was in the same year that FitzGerald published his translation of the *Rubáiyát*, the popularity of which endures to this day.

It seems likely, so Sebald tells us, that Browne would have remained unaware of the strength of his friend's affection and indeed we know of it only because of a note of impassioned condolence that FitzGerald wrote to Browne's widow, a letter which we can only imagine she laid aside 'in amazement if not consternation'. What we know also is that in his declining years FitzGerald suffered from tinnitus, an affliction that prevented him from staging imaginary concerts in what he called the 'Theatre of one's own Recollection'.

FitzGerald died in 1883, before crosswords – which seem increasingly to me to act as a catalyst to my own obscure recollections – were invented. He would not therefore have been troubled by such homophone clues as that offered by Janus last week: 'He wrote Cleopatra's reported reply to Anthony's asking if she was still faithful? (4,7)'.[i]

Gorgeous. Just gorgeous.

20 AUGUST 2004

i OMAR KHAYYÁM

# Guardian *Readers*

From time to time I receive letters from crossword solvers who speculate as to the exact nature of the people who set puzzles for this and other newspapers.* Their undercurrent of gleeful melancholy reminds me of the views of the Hideous Hog in Victor Mollo's peerless books about bridge in 'the Menagerie'. 'You'll find, my friend,' says the Hideous Hog, 'that we are all winners here. Not a loser in sight.' His interlocutor objects that if someone is winning there must, perforce, be someone who is losing. 'A superficial view,' the Hog replies. 'You must be thinking of the money which is purely incidental.' In speech as in bridge the Hog is capable of what we might charitably call spectacular cognitive leaps. 'If people played to win...the game would have come to an end long ago. At Duplicate one pair wins, a few get places and the rest are nowhere. Yet they come up for more punishment again and again. Why? Because bridge is the medium through which they express themselves, each one doing his own thing, odd though it be.'

He compares bridge players favourably with the young who 'disfigure themselves with pink dye' and their elders who 'join societies to inflict compassion on the poor'.

Speaking of whom, I have met several *Guardian* crossword setters and can confirm that they are every bit as devious and duplicitous as my correspondents suggest, although I have yet to meet one who has two heads or one who (as far as I know) has consorted carnally with the devil.

But we more rarely gain insights into what the setters think of us. They must, surely, wonder why we come back day after day for more torment and conclude that we are each doing our own thing, odd though it be? But every now and then they reveal their hand. 'We are inclined to write 'Dear Sir' and argue (8,7)'[i] Araucaria said last week, counting himself amongst our happy but deluded number.

Back in June, Paul kept a discreet distance. 'You are rude and rag is crude (8,7)'[i] he wrote.

\* See p.126–7.

26 AUGUST 2004

i GUARDIAN READERS

## *Leading Folk Astray*

I had the great pleasure this week of meeting Crispa, the *Guardian*'s longest serving setter who had her first puzzle published in the *Radio Times* in 1952 and her first *Guardian* puzzle published in 1954. She is also the first to have composed puzzles simultaneously for all five daily broadsheets, as well as a host of other publications. Others have claimed the distinction, but she argues – with impeccable logic – that, 'As I had puzzle number one in the *Independent*, I must surely have been the first?'

Like many crossword composers – but not all – Crispa keeps meticulous records of all the clues she has composed, cross-referencing them by puzzle, publication and order in which they were used. The filing cabinets that now line the walls of her study are in some sense a social history, reflecting obliquely the passing fashions.

We talked a little about the process of setting puzzles – you are best advised to fill in the long words first, and the right and bottom edges, otherwise you'll find yourself groping around for a nine-letter word ending in 'B'. Of course there are some ('Beelzebub' comes to mind), but that's not the point.

But nor is filling in the grid the most interesting part of composing puzzles. When I asked what it takes to compose crosswords, Crispa rounded up the usual adjectives: fair, witty, entertaining, challenging. She confessed also that for her the best clues were ones that told a story, the ones that had some kind of narrative to them.

Many crossword composers will say the same. What often gets left unsaid in these conversations – perhaps it is too obvious to mention – is that to set crosswords well, you must also be willing to deceive. Crispa said as much in August when she 'Cited many changes that could be misleading (9)',[i] and it was only yesterday that *The Times* (but they don't carry pseudonyms and so I don't know who set the puzzle) was pleased to announce a 'Deft clue I concocted, leading folk astray (9)'.[ii]

24 September 2004

i MENDACITY; ii DECEITFUL

# *Déjà vu*

To understand why Cathy van Starkenburg, a Canadian of Dutch descent, fell off her chair on the morning of 10 November 2004 we have first to understand that she sits on the same chair every morning and that morning in question was no different from any other. It was, so she tells me, a glorious and bright day, as indeed it had been the morning before, with the rising sun filtering through the riot of late autumn colour that filled her part of the Ottawa valley. Her husband had gone off to work at 5.30 a.m., as he always did, which gave her plenty of time to make her toasted cheese and coffee which she always makes the Dutch way, which is to say strong enough that it will make the uninitiated fall off their chairs should they not watch themselves. And, her cheese toasted and her coffee brewed, Cathy sat down to do the *Guardian* crossword puzzle, something she had also done the day before, and the day before that.

For Cathy is a creature of habit and her mornings have taken on a certain regularity ever since she discovered her supply of crosswords. Newspapers are few and far between in her remote farming community, and cryptic puzzles fewer and further, but a couple of years ago Cathy discovered she could get the *Guardian* puzzle via the web. Now it is the first thing she looks for in the morning and her mornings just wouldn't be the same without it. To her delight the puzzle on the morning of 10 November was by Paul, one of her favourite setters.

Before it was time to go to work therefore, she had pretty much knocked it on the head. Only 24 across remained: 'A lesser figure in *Jude the Obscure* – have you read this somewhere before? (4,2).'[i] Which of course she knew she had – at 24 across in the previous day's puzzle by Araucaria.

At which point she fell off her chair laughing and thus changed for ever a morning that had in every other respect been just like the one before.

3 DECEMBER 2004

i DÉJÀ VU

---

## *Araucaria MBE*

If, like me, you sometimes find yourselves doing an anagram with too many or too few letters – if, say, you forget that the 'such' of Screaming Lord Sutch has a 't' in it – then you may have been helped by the tendency I noticed over the holiday period for setters to throw in some Ps and Qs or to drop a few aitches along the way. In the *Week* on Christmas Eve, for example, Tim Moorey began his delightful puzzle with a pre-amble that read, 'The solution to one down clue in each column is one letter too many for the space indicated. Form the grid entry by transferring the extra letter below the grid. This gives a two-word seasonal song whose composer is shown in the shaded squares, reading from left.'

Pasquale went the other way with his entertaining New Year's Day perimetrical, preferring to lose a few letters around the edges. 'The perimeter letters spell out an appropriate message,' his preamble said, 'but these letters are not included in the sub-sidiary indications in the relevant clues.'

With so many stray letters giving so many appropriate messages, I was delighted to find Her Majesty's Government – or was it her Majesty? (one is never quite sure of protocol in these matters, although I am told that the Queen does like a good puzzle) – awarding our most esteemed setter a few letters of his own. Araucaria MBE is, as far as I know, only the second crossword composer to have been so honoured. Apex was the other one, and his citation, like that of Araucaria was 'for services to the newspaper industry'.

Well, perhaps that is what they were serving, but I suspect they and their many fans would see it differently. In Araucaria's case one would have preferred to see what he has done over his forty-six years as a setter described as something else. Services to the delight of others, perhaps, or services to the imagination.

And, as with anagrams sometimes, I did wonder whether HMG had got the right letters?

7 JANUARY 2005

## *Tilting at Windmills*

So many windmills, so little time to tilt!

First there was Virgilius looking for a scrap in the *Independent* last week: 'Guardian showing us it can do with a fixing? (9)'.[i] And then Martin Kelner in the *Guardian*'s very own sports pages. Now, I don't as a general rule like to pick a fight with anyone, let alone my more esteemed colleagues on this newspaper (especially if they're funnier than me), but Monday's slur on the good character of crossword solvers everywhere cannot go unchallenged.

Comparing Formula One press conferences unfavourably with monthly statements on agricultural yield, Kelner then suggested that the drivers who appear at these events 'invariably seem about as thrilled as someone who has just managed to complete the quick crossword in the coffee break'. He meant this pejoratively.

But I know from my considerable postbag on the subject that there are few pleasures in life greater than completing the crossword, quick or otherwise, and during one's coffee break or at any other time, and that people who actually manage this are likely to kiss strangers, pay their taxes or (as was the case with my girlfriend last week) unexpectedly and on a once-only-and-don't-get-any-ideas basis offer to bring one tea in bed.

I had been doing cryptic crosswords for fully seven years before I actually managed to finish one, and in that instance I was so excited I drove off the road and into a passing cow, which then gave every impression of not being amused.

Had Mr Kelner compared Fisichella to the cow, I would have understood.

But perhaps he hasn't read my book.

11 MARCH 2005

i CUSTODIAN

## *Silicone Valley*

To lunch last week with a group of crossword setters and solvers known as 'the Gruntlings'. Many distinguished composers were present, including Dumpynose from the *Spectator* (now why did he choose that pseudonym?), but I was most delighted to meet Roy Dean who sets puzzles for *The Times* and who holds the world record for the fastest verified solution of *The Times* puzzle.

Roy won the first *Times* Crossword Competition in 1970 and decided to take his 'solving speeds' seriously. At the time he was living in Bromley and had a twenty-three-minute train journey into London each day. At first that was his target, but soon he was trying to complete the puzzle before the train reached Brixton, then Herne Hill and so on. He soon reached the point where he would solve the puzzle in the five minutes between arriving at the station and the time his train departed. He wrote to *The Times* saying so, and at 6 a.m. on the day the letter was published, the BBC invited him into the *Today* programme studio to cross swords with Brian Redhead.

And then – without warning – Redhead invited him to solve that morning's puzzle. It was a Saturday, and the puzzle should have been difficult. Roy's heart sank as Redhead started the stopwatch. But an incredible three minutes and forty-five seconds later Roy had completed the puzzle, live on air, and his name was destined for the *Guinness Book of Records*, where it first appeared in 1972.

Roy's delightful book, *Mainly in Fun*, published by The Book Guild, lists some of his favourite clues. But when pressed he drew my attention to this one, which he set in *The Times* in January: 'Silicone Valley? (8)'.[i]

25 MARCH 2005

i CLEAVAGE

# Hitting on the Up

Sometime after my book *Pretty Girl in Crimson Rose (8)*[i] was published a reader wrote to me to say that surely I had the number of letters wrong? It should be (7).[ii] He had spotted that it is one of those rare clues for which there is more than one possible solution. The only deciding factor is the number of letters, like 'Stiff examination (7)' and 'Stiff examination (4,6)'.[iii] The joy of having 'two routes to the solution' is that once you get there, you know it is right. But sometimes – and whether by serendipity or design I cannot say – a clue has two completely legitimate solutions with the same number of letters.

Leaving that aside for the moment I know that you'll be pleased to hear that in my cricket match this week I hit the first ball I faced for six. Whether by design or serendipity remains unclear. The bowler's next ball smacked me on the finger and caused a certain amount of laughter and pain, and for several minutes I confirmed that it is what Araucaria last Wednesday called 'The jumping game (7)'.[iv] Still, I went on to score what I regard as a very respectable total (i.e. more than six) before being stumped trying to belt their spinner over midwicket.

This also caused a certain amount of laughter.

Naturally I took solace in the crossword. Araucaria had themed his Wednesday puzzle on the forthcoming Ashes series, but it was the previous day's Gordius that I found most difficult. I didn't finish it until Carmel Swann wrote to say she and a friend struggled for hours over this clue: 'Trading about a quarter, but it's on the increase (8)'.[v] Well, we all know an anagram when we see one. TRADING + E. The solution was obviously GRADIENT.

Except it wasn't. He was talking about my finger.

I wonder if he meant it.

8 JULY 2005

i REBELLED; ii REDDISH; iii AUTOPSY and POST MORTEM respectively;

iv CRICKET; v SWELLING

---

## On Writing

For much of this summer the men's pond on Hampstead Heath has been closed. Apparently blooming blue-green algae (I'm told this is a technical term) has made it unsafe for swimming. As a result I find I make fewer early-morning pilgrimages to my favourite part of London. But I like the early mornings and yesterday I found myself watching the sun rise over Giancarlo Neri's sculpture, 'The Writer'. The nine-metre high table and chair rises from the dry grasses of the Heath.

According to its creator, it is a tribute to the 'loneliness of the writer'. Neri is quoted as saying, '"The Writer" was prompted by the idea of the writer's condition: that in order to write about people and life, they actually have to set themselves apart… It's as ordinary as possible. I think of it as a stage set waiting for actors who never come.'

Except they do come. They see it and climb it, make love under it and throw balls over it. They use it for goalposts and shade. Dogs pee on it and foxes pause beneath it. Yesterday's fox seemed unconcerned by my presence. He – I think it was a 'he', though how do you tell? – sniffed around the edges before drifting off towards the south meadow.

I am not convinced by the need for writers to set themselves apart. It seems more likely that in order to write about 'people and life' we have to immerse ourselves in them and it. Louise MacNeice is the model. He 'would have a poet able-bodied, fond of talking, a reader of the newspapers, capable of pity and laughter, informed in economics, appreciative of women, involved in personal relationships, actively interested in politics, susceptible to physical impressions…'

Otherwise it's just, 'The ego-trip of a writer (6)'.[i]

15 JULY 2005

i GOETHE by Rufus. Actually he had 'German writer' as the definition.

---

# *A Scrupulous Confession*

As confessions go, it seems modest enough. 'Perhaps one warning might be given,' Araucaria writes in his introduction to *Araucaria Crosswords Volume 2* (Chambers 2005). 'I find that in those days I was less scrupulous than I am now about the indication of anagrams.'

The 'days' to which he refers are the mid 1980s when he (and later Enigmatist) edited *1 Across*, a magazine of puzzles for those who found insufficient torment in their daily crossword. It was also a place where setters could 'have more fun', he told me when I called to ask. In part the 'fun' consists of experimenting with grids. But there is also a sense that those who subscribe to the magazine expect the setters to stray a little outside the rules.

It is permissible to 'be a little more eccentric' in their clueing, and to do it secure in the knowledge that there will not be a barrage of complaint from solvers.

What the setter can also experiment with are the instructions and this new collection contains as fine a set of eye-glazing preambles as one could wish to meet. They range from the very droll: 'It will be observed that the number of spaces available for each solution is greater than the number in brackets after its clue…' to the downright obscure: 'Many means for getting across, including more than one for some acrosses, have vanished.'

I was relieved to see that, despite my recent sojourn on the Pelion Peninsula, the puzzle entitled 'Greek Alphabetical Puzzle' has a preamble that reads, 'Knowledge of Greek is not required.' Well, thank goodness for that; it turns out that the alphabet in question is the Greek one. And I couldn't help feeling that in the midst of all this a slightly obscure anagram indicator was not going to put anyone off.

The magazine is now twenty-one years old and still going strong. Readers who want a sample copy (before deciding to subscribe!) should send a self-addressed c5 envelope to *1 Across*, The Old Chapel, Middleton Tyas, Richmond, North Yorkshire, DL10 6PP.

26 AUGUST 2005

# THE OMNIBUS PUZZLE

# *To or For, By With or From Everybody*

It is not often a new setter swims into our ken. In recent times only Brummie, whose work also appears in *Private Eye* under the pseudonym Cyclops, has made it into the hallowed company of *Guardian* setters. But on 29 August 2005 solvers were treated to a new puzzle by a setter calling him or herself, Omnibus, which, if my schoolboy Latin serves me, means 'to or for, by with or from everybody'.

Which indeed it was. All through the spring and summer of 2005 X-Philes readers composed clues for words I selected. The composer of the clue that I found 'most delightful' – a wholly subjective and sometimes infuriating judgement that, if their letters were to be believed, drove more than one setter to drink – won a box of Divine chocolate and their clue was included in the following puzzle. Hugh Stephenson, crossword editor at the *Guardian*, agreed to run the puzzle and a new setter was born. I, for one, took great delight in enabling so many solvers to share their ingenuity with their fellow *Guardian* readers.

There was only the briefest preamble: 'The clues to this puzzle have been contributed by 2 down.'

To all of whom I am very grateful.

## Guardian Puzzle 23,545

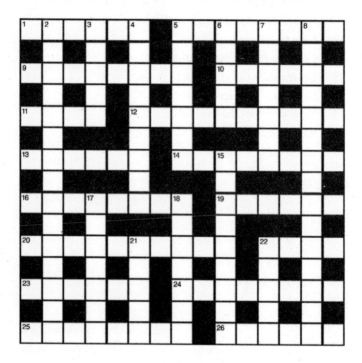

By Omnibus

**Across**

1     Fire back through the fleeting image (6)

5     Odd fetish is most suspect (8)

9     Distorted view that on average everyone gets a ten (8)

10    Lunatic can sue for terms of payment (6)

11    Ladies out to lunch *might* be represented as this (4)

12    Her pal or his? (10)

13   Grandmaster's opening? To an extent (6)

14   Industrial theory used to arrest Swiss in incest scandal (8)

16   Outlaw Charles as King? Mail in frenzy! (8)

19   Note to taxman – 'Get a life!' (6)

20   Like Loman, but no Willy! (10)

22   Some bimbo dying for congress, perhaps (4)

23   Celebrate - perhaps with this car? (6)

24   Go east. Adopt the persecuted (6,2)

25   Providing a choice like kind newspaper man (8)

26   Mock the German and die, strangely (6)

## Down

2   Delusions of grandeur are said to become us (8,7)

3   To give this in an enema would be daft (5)

4   Teach development in the glen (9)

5   Stands for Fiona's first dance (7)

6   Starts to swing club up – 'Fore!' – finishes in rough (5)

7   I get little thanks putting stud back in Berlusconi's tongue (7)

8   Gaga? Mad! Hi, Doc, hold on a tick! (6,9)

15   Stick? Stick! Stick for concrete (6,3)

17   Conductor? Vanessa's trio does without one! (7)

18   Poor company? (7)

21   What eats mouse-tail and has ears? (5)

22   Not bright of King to follow Blair's lead? (5)

**Solution to puzzle 23,545**

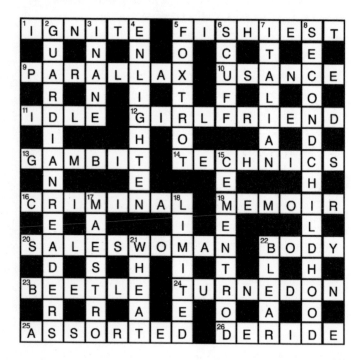

The setters: Richard Crouch, Erica Cox, Carol de Rose, Neil Leach, Barbara Langley, Rob Hick, Kim Taplin, Dave Tilley, Tim Moorey, Michael Bulley, Richard Saunders, Peter Evans, Tom Sharpe, Peter Smyth, Bob Ayton, Nicky Clark, Jen Smyth, Robin Gilbert, Jessica Meek, Alison Prince, Peter Brunner, John Whitehead.

# Epilogue

# *I Say Nothing*

If, like me, you occasionally put nuggets of your modest life into the public domain you will sooner or later be asked how you remember it all. 'Do you keep a diary?' people will say when what they really mean is, 'Why the hell should we believe you?'

The answer to the diary question is yes and no. I don't keep one but I do keep books in which I write daily letters to each of my children. And I have notebooks – random, cryptic, chaotic, piecemeal notebooks. The notes are often undated and always fragmentary. They cover inscriptions on park benches, conversations overheard, and the price of petrol in Brighton. (Why more than in Archway? Was it just that particular garage?) And they are all handwritten, which gives them a particular power as *aides memoir*. Was that ink smudged by a raindrop or a tear? And whose tear was it?

Why do we do it? Many others have been here before. I often return to Joan Didion's essay 'On Keeping a Notebook'. 'The point of keeping a notebook has never been, nor is it now, to have an accurate factual record of what I have been doing or thinking,' she wrote. 'That would be a different impulse entirely, an instinct for reality which I sometimes envy but do not possess.' Didion concludes that the reason we do it is this: 'Remember what it was to be me: that is always the point. It is a difficult point to admit. We are brought up in the ethic that others, any others, all others, are more interesting than ourselves...'

And even though we disagree, we don't like to admit it. Which is why when people ask why I keep notes and why I write about myself in the public domain, it seems to me the safest and truest answer is, 'I say nothing (3)'.[i]

9 SEPTEMBER 2005

i EGO by Enigmatist.

___